Educating Citizens
for
Global Awareness

Educating Citizens

for

Global Awareness

edited by

NEL NODDINGS

developed in association
with the Boston Research Center
for the 21st Century

Teachers College
Columbia University
New York and London

Published by Teachers College Press, 1234 Amsterdam Avenue, New York, NY 10027

Copyright © 2005 by Boston Research Center for the 21st Century

Library of Congress Cataloging-in-Publication Data

Educating citizens for global awareness / edited by Nel Noddings.
    p. cm.
  Includes bibliographical references and index.
    ISBN 0-8077-4535-9 (cloth : alk. paper) — ISBN 0-8077-4534-0 (pbk. : alk. paper)
    1. International education—United States. 2. World citizenship—Study and teaching—United States. I. Noddings, Nel.

  LC1090.E225 2004
  370.116—dc22

2004058061

ISBN 0-8077-4534-0 (paper)
ISBN 0-8077-4535-9 (cloth)

Printed on acid-free paper

Manufactured in the United States of America

12 11 10 09 08 07 06 05 8 7 6 5 4 3 2 1

About the Boston Research Center

This work is published in association with **The Boston Research Center for the 21st Century**, an international peace institute that envisions a worldwide network of global citizens developing cultures of peace through dialogue and understanding. We believe that the best hope for the realization of this vision is through the active cultivation of an inclusive sense of community, locally and globally.

This process of cultivation is grounded in three values that are essential to cultures of peace: *wisdom* to perceive the interconnectedness of all life; *courage* not to fear but to respect differences and strive to learn from people of different cultures; and *compassion* that extends beyond the near and familiar to all those suffering far away. The Center's strategic framework for cultivating a sense of inclusive community rests on three pillars: the promotion of women's leadership for peace, support for education for global citizenship, and the development of a philosophy and practice of community through dialogue. We sponsor public forums, educational seminars, and peacemaking circles that are collaborative, diverse, and intergenerational. Our publications include a semiannual newsletter, a resource-packed Web site, and multiauthor books, which provide curricular support for university courses in ethics, peace studies, education, and comparative religion. BRC books have been adopted by professors in over 100 American colleges and universities for use in more than 200 courses to date. Order information can be found at www.brc21.org.

The Center was founded in 1993 by Daisaku Ikeda, a peace activist and president of Soka Gakkai International (SGI), a Buddhist association with members in 187 countries.

The Boston Research Center is located at 396 Harvard Street, Cambridge, MA 02138. Tel: 617-491-1090; Fax: 617-491-1169; E-mail: center@brc21.org; Web site: www.brc21.org.

Project Manager: Patti M. Marxsen

Developmental editing: Helen Marie Casey

Contents

Foreword

THE SEPTEMBER 11, 2001, TERRORIST ATTACKS in the United States were a grave challenge to the ideal of dialogue between civilizations, the quest on which the world embarked at the start of the new century. They were acts of wanton mayhem that threatened to undermine humanity's most basic right to live in peace. It is my belief that the eradication of terrorism calls for the creation of new, international political, legal, and economic systems, as well as security measures. But it cannot stop there. Ultimately, the challenge must be taken up in terms of our understanding and approach to human civilization itself.

The great wave of globalization sweeping contemporary society, in areas such as information and communications, science and technology, and the market economy, is a contrast of light and dark. The positive potentials are democratization and the spread of awareness of human rights; the negative aspects are war and conflict, rising economic disparities, the obliteration of distinctive cultures, the spread of weapons of mass destruction, and the destruction of the global ecology.

These dark shadows entailed in the current process of globalization stir a vortex of malice and mistrust and provoke an identity crisis in the very depths of the human spirit. Only as a growing movement of people work to transform this bleak spiritual landscape will specific, concrete measures produce meaningful results at the international level.

Education, in the genuine sense of the word, holds the key to resolving these problems. Education has the power to enrich the inner landscape of the human spirit, to build within people's hearts what the Constitution of the United Nations Educational, Scientific and Cultural Organization (UNESCO) refers to as "the defenses of peace." True education summons forth the innate goodness of humanity—our capacity for nonviolence, trust, and benevolence. It enables individuals to reveal their unique qualities and, by encouraging empathy with others, opens the door to the peaceful coexistence of humanity. This kind of humanistic education is crucial if we are to foster global citizens.

In Buddhism, the creative harmonization of diversity is expressed through an analogy with various flowering trees: the cherry, plum, peach, and damson. Like these trees, we are each replete with our particular characteristics and possibilities. It is by mutually recognizing and respecting these differences that the unique capacities of each individual can be brought to full and equal bloom, ultimately creating a beautiful, peaceful, and harmonious world. This understanding and appreciation of interdependence is referred to as "dependent origination" in Buddhism.

I believe that three qualities in particular are required of global citizens:

The first is wisdom—the ability to perceive the interdependence of all life. In Buddhism, this is referred to as the wisdom of dependent origination.

The second is courage—the courage to respect one anothers' differences and use them as an impetus to creative living, rather than rejecting or excluding others on the basis of differences of culture, nationality, and race. In the Buddhist tradition, this is embodied in the character of the bodhisattva, "Bestower of Fearlessness."

The third is the ability to empathize with and share the pain of every person and all of life. In Buddhism, this is the ideal of compassion, which means being a true friend who hears the anguished cries of others, striving with them to overcome and surmount suffering.

Humanistic education must foster people of character, people who are richly endowed with these qualities of wisdom, courage, and compassion. Its aim must be to form global citizens committed to an indivisible solidarity of human happiness, one that embraces all members of our species.

In specific terms, how should we encourage global citizenship?

Tsunesaburo Makiguchi (1871–1944), the first president of the Soka Gakkai, developed the idea of an educational process rooted in, and starting from, the local community and extending its scope of concern to the national and ultimately the global level. Makiguchi rejected both narrow-minded nationalism and the kind of globalism that lacks concrete content. He stressed that the education of global citizens must start at the level of the local community, extending outward from there.

True education consists of revealing and demonstrating the core principles required for global citizenship within the context of local community. In *A Geography of Human Life* (1903/2002), Makiguchi urged that community education should not only hone the powers of scientific observation and understanding, but should also develop public-spiritedness, as well as sensitive awareness of moral and religious perspectives.

Makiguchi considered the identity of a global citizen on the three levels of local, national, and global community, and showed that the character of a global citizen is created through a dynamic harmonization and development of these three levels. As the individual grows, the sphere of what that individual experiences as her or his local community expands to a national and then global scale. Thus, humanitarian contributions to one's community and country further the cause of world peace; at the same time, contributions to global humanity on a planetary level reverberate back to the national and local levels.

Makiguchi argued that the ultimate purpose of the state is, therefore, the pursuit of the prosperity of human civilization and the advancement of human reason. To this end, states should shift from competition in the military, political, and economic spheres to what he terms a "humanitarian competition" of contribution to human happiness.

The key to the formation of global citizens is the educator, bearing out the concept that the teacher is the most important element in the educational environment. Within the interaction between different personalities—as individual human beings, as teacher and learner—the enormous potential hidden in the deepest realms of life itself may be fully developed. In that sense, I am convinced that this volume will provide a major contribution to the development of the education of global citizens.

Finally, I would like to express my heartfelt gratitude to Dr. Nel Noddings, whose work has focused on research into the ethics of care and spiritual education, and the distinguished scholars from various fields who have penned articles for this volume.

Daisaku Ikeda
Founder, Boston Research Center for the 21st Century
President, Soka Gakkai International

Preface

IN JUNE 2003, A GLOBAL ATTITUDES SURVEY, "Views of a Changing World," released by Pew Research Center for the People and the Press, documented "a widespread belief among people in most nations that their culture is superior to others." United States citizens were in the forefront. The survey stated, "Among wealthy nations, Americans stand out for their sense of cultural superiority. Six in ten people in the United States agree with the statement: 'Our people are not perfect, but our culture is superior to others' (p. 93)." Clearly, education for global citizenship is needed throughout the world, and especially in the United States. This volume is intended to help meet that need.

In the concluding chapter, editor Nel Noddings advises educators to resist the temptation to put the full responsibility for citizenship education on social studies educators. She points to the many opportunities for teaching better global attitudes in, for example, science, literature, and even math classes. In spite of a curriculum stressed by the current testing mania, there are middle school and high school teachers who are reaching out to enrich their courses with global content. This book is meant not just for these already-aware teachers, but also for teachers and would-be teachers who are skeptics, those who might ask: What is global citizenship? Is it just a slogan? Why should I make time for this . . . and how? This book begins to answer such questions and, under the guidance of Nel Noddings, it proceeds with the necessary humility. In her closing words, she envisions teachers engaging students in "open, honest dialogue—sharing, guiding, and staying with them as they struggle with problems we have not solved."

The inspiration for this book comes from Boston Research Center's founder, Daisaku Ikeda, who has dedicated his life to education in its highest sense. We feel privileged to have had an opportunity to work with philosopher-educator Nel Noddings, whose groundbreaking work on caring education and feminist ethics we deeply admire. She brought wide-ranging experience, practical wisdom, and a critical intelligence to this project, along with a good dose of humor and patience. With Nel's help we engaged essays from a diverse group of creative educators whose thoughtful contributions have succeeded in proving the point she makes in her introduction, that global citizenship cannot be defined from only one vantage point.

Project manager extraordinaire Patti Marxsen not only did a magnificent job of bringing harmony out of chaos whenever it threatened, but also went the extra mile. Having become fully immersed and fascinated with the subject herself, Patti composed an invaluable resource for teachers who may be inspired to put the insights of this volume into action. In the *Resources* section of the BRC website, www.brc21.org, thanks to Patti's good efforts, we now offer a link to "Curriculum Resources for Global Citizenship Education." Helen Casey, our trusted companion on all of our publishing projects to date, has once again brought her way with words to the making of this book. We are grateful to the distinguished Teachers College Press for working with us to refine our initial plans and signing on as our publishing partner.

May this book support teachers in awakening young Americans to genuine global concerns.

Virginia Straus
Executive Director
Boston Research Center for the 21st Century

Global Citizenship: Promises and Problems

Nel Noddings

My country is the world; to do good is my religion.
—Thomas Paine

ON A RECENT DAY, I SENT e-mail messages to people in Japan, Argentina, the Netherlands, and England. Before I finished reading my own messages, I had an automatic response from the recipient in England, telling me that he was in Ethiopia and would respond to the substance of my message later. In a world of instant communication and swift travel, we have become keenly aware of our interdependence. Many of us are now concerned about the welfare of all human and nonhuman life, preservation of the Earth as home to that life, and the growing conflict between the appreciation of diversity and the longing for unity. We are concerned, too, that our technological capacity has run far beyond our moral competence to manage it. We dream of peace in a world perpetually on the edge of war. One response to these concerns is the promotion of global citizenship.

But what do we mean by *global citizenship?* This is not an easy question to answer, and the issues that arise as we try to answer it are difficult. However, even if we cannot answer the question entirely to our satisfaction, these issues belong in discussions of schooling practices and curriculum. In what follows, I first explore the basic question: What is *global citizenship?* Then I look more closely at four of the issues that arise from the initial exploration: Is global citizenship primarily a matter of economics? How can we protect the Earth as our home and that of future generations? What sort of diversity should we try to preserve, and can we encourage unity while we

1

maintain diversity? What role should peace education play in promoting global citizenship?

WHAT IS GLOBAL CITIZENSHIP?

The words *citizenship* and *citizen* usually refer to a national or regional identity. One who is recognized as a citizen of a particular nation has the special rights and duties prescribed by the government of that nation. Global citizenship cannot yet be described in this way. There is no global government to which we as individuals owe allegiance, and there are no international laws that bind us unless our national government accepts them. Thus, we can't look to the familiar, technical definition of citizenship to help us in describing global citizenship.

Sometimes *citizen* is used synonymously with *inhabitant*, as in "the deer is a citizen of the forest." Although this statement is charming, most of us think that citizenship involves more than a reference to where we live and even more than the technical description of our national (or regional) rights and responsibilities. Educators have been trying for years to describe citizenship more fully and to figure out ways to promote it. For example, some social studies educators believe that the study of American history promotes American citizenship (Thornton 2001b). Does it? To answer this question, we have to say much more about what is meant by citizenship. In her chapter in this volume, Gloria Ladson-Billings points out that even within a nation, some of those who qualify formally for citizenship do not feel as though they share fully in that citizenship.

Perhaps we can agree that a citizen of Place X has (or should have) an interest in, or concern about, the welfare of X and its people. Such a citizen cares about X and wants to protect its interests and way of life. This is a description with which Americans are familiar, and it is used often to arouse national pride and commitment. It would take us too far afield to explore all the ways in which people have described "American interests" and the "American way of life." But we know that attempts at such description exhibit complexity and conflict. It is not an easy job to say exactly what is meant by "the" American way of life. We fall easily into slogans and clichés.

Consider, then, how much harder it will be to define global citizenship. Is there, for example, a global way of life? Some think that there could be—even that there should be—a global way of life, and it usually looks suspiciously like their own way. Advocates of globalization—"the removal of barriers to free trade and the closer integration of national economies" (Stiglitz 2002, ix)—come close to defining global citizenship solely in terms of economics. A global citizen, from this perspective, is one who can live and work effectively anywhere in the world, and a global way of life would both describe and support the functioning of global citizens.

Many careful thinkers are critical of this approach, and international meetings of world financial organizations have been marked by riotous protests. What sparks the protests? What are the objections to globalization? First, there is evidence that present efforts at globalization have aggravated existing economic injustice. Good global citizens should be concerned about this, just as good national citizens are concerned about injustice within their own boundaries. This observation prompts us to think more about the idea of *interest*. It may be better for present purposes to use *concern* instead of *interest*. *Interest* too often conveys the notion of self-interest or concentration on the benefits to one's own group. Indeed, when citizens of one nation speak of their *interests*, people of other nations are understandably wary. When our interests are truly global, this worry should be relieved. But for now, to avoid this problem, let's speak of *concern*. When we are concerned with the welfare of X—our nation, region, or globe—we are concerned with the well-being of all its inhabitants.

Second, globalization's emphasis on economic growth has led to practices that threaten the physical environment—the life of the Earth itself. The problems in this area are so complex that even scientists are unsure about the harms and benefits resulting from certain practices. It seems clear that global warming is a reality and that the reduction of carbon emissions is imperative. However, other practices—the genetic engineering of plants, for example—need much more study. Closely related to problems concerning the global environment are those that affect people in particular locations. What may be good for people in a large region (say, a huge dam designed to provide electricity) may be a disaster for those in the particular locality. Some global citizens may be willing to live anywhere, but others want to live in a particular place that they love. Is love of place compatible with global citizenship? At the very least, we've added another factor to the concerns of global citizens—the well-being of particular physical places.

Third, critics object to construing global interest entirely in economic terms. Even if it were possible and just to establish one world economic order, other aspects of life must be considered. If global citizens appreciate cultural diversity, they will speak of *ways* of life, not one way, and they will ask how a valued diversity can be maintained. But what sorts of diversity should we appreciate? If a culture wants to maintain the inequality of women or the slavery of children, should we accept these practices as tolerable facets of cultural diversity—as simply "their way"? When cultural diversity pushes us toward moral relativism, we must back away. And so we have to think carefully about the merits of diversity and those of unity or universality and how to achieve an optimal balance between the two. We should be interested in social as well as economic justice.

Fourth, because globalization points to a global economy, we have to ask whose economic vision will be adopted. As noted earlier, the powerful nations are likely to impose their own vision. At the present time, the most powerful view is that of the huge international corporations. Even if it could be argued that their vision is benign and requires only tinkering to be just, many of the world's people harbor doubts, and while the disparity between rich and poor grows, it is predictable that groups (even nations) will protest violently. Moreover, nations of the First World often associate corporate capitalism with their own overall way of life, and this association adds a strong ideological component to the problem. Citizens of wealthy nations may feel it a patriotic duty to defend economic practices that seem inseparable from their way of life. These citizens then try to persuade or even force others to accept that way of life "for their own good."

We must ask, also, whether global citizenship—defined in part as the activation of the concerns so far identified—is compatible with national citizenship. Should we put the concerns of globe or nation first, or is this a bad question? Should our choice depend on the particular concern under consideration? Is there an inherent conflict between patriotism and global citizenship? Can patriotism be redefined in a way that removes the conflict?

It would seem that peace is a precondition of global citizenship. I cannot be a global citizen if my country is at war with others, any more than a loyal citizen of Virginia could be a U.S. citizen during the Civil War. One could argue, of course, that a progressive orientation toward global citizenship will promote world peace. This is a chicken-and-egg argument. However we arrange the priorities, peace education must play a vital role in the promotion of global citizenship. A global citizen must see war as contrary to all of the concerns we have identified—to worldwide economic and social justice, to the health of our physical world, to the preservation of well-loved places, to the balance of diversity and unity, and to the well-being of all of earth's inhabitants. Yet if war comes, the vast majority of us will stand— sadly, perhaps even angrily—with our own nation. Even our enemies, educated as badly as we are, would think less of us if we did not. This underscores our earlier claim that war cannot be reconciled with global concerns, and so peace education must play a vital role in supporting global citizenship.

Before exploring some of these issues in greater depth, we should return briefly to the question of what can be learned from our experience in educating for national citizenship. I mentioned earlier that some educators believe that the teaching of American history promotes American citizenship. As Thornton (2001b) has shown, there is little evidence to support this belief. Perhaps we need a blend of history, geography, civics, and other studies to encourage good citizenship. Perhaps no amount of knowledge will accomplish that goal. We may need forms of practice and participation that we rarely offer in schools. Still, it seems clear that knowledge must inform practice. As we look at the issues involved in global citizenship, we must try to identify the knowledge and skills students will need to achieve this new form of citizenship.

ECONOMIC AND SOCIAL JUSTICE

One deep concern of good citizens is economic justice. Global citizenship requires a commitment to the elimination of poverty. Joseph Stiglitz notes that the motto of the World Bank is "Our dream is a world without poverty" (Stiglitz 2002, 23). The World Bank and other global organizations (for example, the International Monetary Fund and the World Trade Organization) have accomplished some noteworthy goals, but they have not eliminated poverty, and some of their practices have actually increased it. Because the people who run these organizations are trained in and committed to the economic theories associated with capitalism, they think in terms of growth. But growth, measured by an increase in national wealth, does not always reduce poverty. To do so, policymakers must select strategies deliberately designed to manage growth in ways that reduce poverty. The perceived failure of world financial organizations to do this has motivated the fierce opposition to them that we saw in Seattle, Washington, Genoa, and Canada.

I have already outlined some important objections to globalization. Of crucial importance is the complaint that globalization as it has been defined by the World Bank, IMF, and WTO has increased the misery of many people (Bigelow and Peterson 2002). Critics condemn, among other things, the continued (and abusive) use of child labor and the existence of sweatshops in developing nations. Whether the overall picture is as bad as that depicted by protestors is not clear (Singer 2002), but it can be shown that some particular situations are very bad indeed.

This observation should alert us to a difficult issue for educators. We often seek numbers or statistics to back our positions, but numbers can be notoriously misleading. We may be able to show, for example, that a nation has experienced a substantial increase in growth; at the same time, other numbers tell us that the gap between rich and poor in that nation has also increased greatly. Which numbers are more important? If the condition of the poor has improved despite the gap, should the gap itself be a concern? There are both short- and long-term views to consider. Might current poverty be a temporary price to pay as growth is encouraged? Eventually, some insist, growth will better the condition of everyone. This is at least questionable.

Teachers who want to help their students to understand the deceptive possibilities of numbers might use a strategy that alternates between global figures and those closer to home. For example, students are often told that jobs in the future will require a great deal of education. This is a reason given for students to stay in school and study hard. But is it true? Many of the fastest-growing jobs (measured by percentage of growth) do indeed require a college-level education. But the fastest growing jobs are not the ones that will employ the most workers. One has to look at the base as well as the percentage of growth. The occupations that will employ most workers in the next decade are almost all jobs that require little education (see Bracey 2003; Noddings 2003a).

Students should learn to look at numerical data carefully. They should, of course, ask about the source of figures. Who provides them, and might there be a hidden agenda in what is presented? Further, they should be encouraged to dig more deeply behind the figures. Suppose a nation reports fewer people living in poverty in 2002 than in 1998. That certainly looks good. But what if the condition of those who remain in poverty has worsened dramatically? And what if those who are living well clearly have the resources to help and yet do nothing?

Conditions in poorer nations, as described in *Rethinking Globalization* (Bigelow and Peterson 2002), are truly dreadful: high infant mortality, starvation, exploitation of workers in sweatshops, destruction of the natural environment, lack of medicines for preventable and curable diseases, child labor, deprivation of education. Any sensitive person—any global citizen—reading this list will be moved to say that something must be done.

But who should act and how? Peter Singer (2002) argues that the wealthy nations, especially the United States, should do much more to relieve starvation and suffering in poor countries. This seems unarguable. However, Singer goes on to argue that if governments do not provide adequate help, individuals should do so, and he insists that "hundreds of millions of people" can afford to give $200 a year to overseas aid and yet are not doing so (Singer 2002, 188). What Singer overlooks is that America ranks in the top three of advanced democracies in charitable giving and volunteerism (Halstead 2003, 124). According to the same source (which students should check), it also ranks in the bottom three (worst) in poverty, economic inequality, infant mortality, health care coverage, life expectancy, and personal savings. Much needs to be done right here in the United States. It may be that Americans have made choices different from the ones advocated by Singer for their charitable giving.

The debate over who should act and how might be a lively one. Some students may argue that "charity begins at home." To this Singer would no doubt point out that he is talking about *starvation and death*, not the satisfaction of selfish wants and minor needs. Should we let children in Africa starve so that students in our own town can have new band uniforms? Put so starkly, the choice seems obvious. But suppose kids in our town or the next one really need more food, heat in their houses and schoolrooms, dental care, protection from adult abuse, and winter clothing? (See Kozol 1991.) The needs all over the world, including the United States, are enormous.

There are better arguments against Singer's demands, however, than the one that says, "charity begins at home" (which he has wrongly attributed to me—see Singer 2002, 159). We really cannot *care for* people at a great distance without some means of direct contact. *Caring for*, as I have described it (Noddings 1984, 2002), requires us to respond to expressed needs and to monitor the effects of our actions and react anew to the responses of those we care for. This does not mean that we cannot *care about* many people for whom we cannot care directly. *Caring about* requires us to work toward the establishment of conditions under which *caring for* can flourish. This is exactly the professed attitude of the large world economic organizations, but—as we have seen—mistakes can be made, and greed can displace the professed attitude and its goals.

The demands of *caring for* involve not only immediate response (someone on the spot must provide food now) but also concern for the future. This kind of direct caring has for centuries been the primary responsibility of women but, as Peggy McIntosh reminds us in her chapter, it has not been highly valued in the arena of public affairs. *Caring for* stays with the cared-for. If I save a child from starvation today, what will prevent her starving tomorrow? What will prevent his becoming a victim or perpetrator of atrocious violence? How will he or she be educated? All of these questions point to the need for the establishment and maintenance of environments in which caring can be effective. What can we do in this direction? We might vote for candidates who endorse the world organizations that operate most effectively on the global plane. We might seek out charitable organizations that are working not only to meet emergencies but also to create long-term conditions for the well-being of those now suffering. Clearly, learning how to conduct ourselves as global citizen-carers is a major educational task.

In addition to finding the right candidates and organizations to support, we should examine our own ways of life. Almost certainly the present way of life in the United States is not sustainable. We consume far too great a proportion of the world's resources, and it seems unlikely that everyone, everywhere, could live as middle-class Americans now live. Should we change, or is this assessment simply wrong? Here we have to be practical while trying to create a sustainable way of life. If we were all to adopt a simple, frugal way of life tomorrow, the American financial world would collapse, and quite possibly the least well off among us would suffer the most. Life as we know it in the United States seems to depend on the willingness of consumers to continue spending. We should, however, be able at least to move toward a more sustainable way of life. Happiness does not depend on wealth. Indeed, economists and social scientists have shown that beyond the poverty level, more money does not correlate with a higher level of happiness (Lane 2000). This is an important message for students to hear.

Dare we ask our students to consider adopting economic moderation as a virtue? Some years ago, in a course I was teaching on moral education, I raised this question. Many students answered affirmatively, and they went on to declare that no individual needs a yearly income in the millions. While suggesting moderation, no one in the class made the kind of demands for individual sacrifice that Singer has made. Certainly no one suggested a legal limit on incomes such as one suggested years ago by George Orwell (1941)—that the highest income not be allowed to exceed the lowest by more than 10 times and that anything in excess of that amount should be taxed at 100%! We were expressing a positive view of voluntary moderation as a personal and national virtue. Yet two students expressed outrage. No way were they willing to put voluntary limits on what they could acquire through their own efforts. That conversation is one I'll never forget. Steeped in Horatio Alger tales of poor boys rising through hard work to positions of wealth and power, many of us in the United States find it incredible—even unpatriotic—to suggest that this way of life should be modified.

There is another objection to the severe demands made by Orwell and Singer. When compassionate response is made a matter of duty and obligation, there will be resistance. We may squirm with guilt, but then we begin to look for arguments that will excuse us. It may be that most kind people will respond with aid to misery when they feel able to do so. When helping adds to our own happiness, as it often does when we care directly and see the positive results of our caring, we are more likely to continue our efforts (Noddings 2003a). We are different individuals, with different temperaments and talents, leading different lives with different resources and obligations. Under any workable moral code, we should be allowed to choose the arenas in which we will concentrate our care. Our choices will, of course, be guided by the severity of needs. Dorothy Day, who lived her life in solidarity with the poor, never made her caring into a grim duty. She said that we must "keep in mind the duty of delight" (Day 1952, 285). I would prefer "possibility" or "gift" to "duty," but her point is important. Caring for, about, and with others can add to our own happiness. We might even call this an ecological view of caring.

The concerns of global citizens extend beyond economic justice to social/political justice. Rights that we demand for ourselves should be offered to others worldwide. The charter of the United Nations refers to "fundamental human rights," to the "dignity and worth of the human person," and to the "equal rights of men and women and of nations large and small." Its Universal Declaration of Human Rights was adopted in 1948 and should be studied by all aspiring global citizens. Similarly, students should know something about the United Nations Declaration of the Rights of the Child (United Nations 1959). The world has fallen pitifully short of upholding these ideals (Bigelow and Peterson 2002).

The analysis of social/political rights is, like the other concerns we have discussed, marked by complexity. It is generous and just to extend important rights to all of the world's people. But suppose some people reject one or another of these rights? Rights arise out of expressed needs (Noddings 2002), and different cultures put emphasis on different needs. Moreover, when basic needs are unsatisfied, some rights taken for granted by citizens of advanced democracies may seem frivolous. Should we force our own ideal of rights on others?

Isaiah Berlin (1969) advised caution in deciding for others what is in their best interest. Sometimes, because we are in positions of knowledge and power, we feel justified in coercing others "for their own sake." Berlin cautions, "I am then claiming that I know what they truly need better than they know it themselves" (1969, 133). If this goes too far, he writes:

> I am in a position to ignore the actual wishes of men or societies, to bully, oppress, torture them in the name . . . of their "real" selves, in the secure knowledge that whatever is the true goal of man (happiness, performance of duty, wisdom, a just society, self-fulfillment) must be identical with his freedom . . . (1969, p. 133)

These are important cautionary words and remind us that people or nations may not be grateful when we insist on liberating them by force or imposing the wonders of modernization on them. A guiding principle for both economic and social justice is suggested by Stiglitz:

> Those whose lives will be affected by the decisions about how globalization is managed have a right to participate in that debate, and they have a right to know how such decisions have been made in the past. (2002, p. xvi)

This last comment underscores the importance of *caring for*—the heart of which is listening and responding to what is there. We should certainly offer to extend our own concept of justice and, when it is endorsed by others, we should work to make it a reality. But we should work together. Global citizenship cannot be defined from a single viewpoint.

PROTECTING THE EARTH

Protecting the Earth is one of the most important tasks facing global citizens. Without a hospitable physical environment, we will live with increasing discomfort and, perhaps, even meet extinction. As we consider how to tackle this task, we will encounter several familiar themes, among them greed and lack of moderation.

Greed is certainly one motivation for acts that endanger the earth. Chandra Muzaffar comments:

> In pursuit of quick profits, corporations, big and small, in different parts of the world have, in the last one hundred years, engaged in indiscriminate logging, thus reducing forest cover; corporations have polluted rivers and oceans, poisoned the air, and threatened fish, insects, mammals, and birds with extinction. Even the lives of the "haves" are contributing toward environmental degradation. (Knitter and Muzaffar 2002, 158)

Greed is clearly one factor to blame for destructive human activity, but it is not the only one. Sometimes, pressed by growing human needs, we simply make mistakes, or we solve one problem only to find that we have created another. The construction of huge dams on some rivers is an example. One result has been an increase in much-needed electric power benefiting many people; another, negative result has been widespread pollution of irrigated land, enormous reduction in the population of certain fish, and the destruction of wildlife habitats (Reisner 1993; Steinberg 2002; Ward 2002). To be sure, there are tales of greed in the history of competition for land, water, and power, but there are also tales of ignorance and clumsy experimentation.

Consider another example. The so-called "Green Revolution" that swept the world in the mid-20th century made it possible to feed a rapidly growing population. The methods of the Green Revolution were not foisted on an unwilling Third World. They were eagerly embraced by nations facing economic problems and, in some cases, even widespread hunger, and the new methods did lead to greatly increased agricultural yields. However, the Green Revolution also had "troubling side effects" (Steinberg 2002, 270), among them the overuse of fertilizers, increase in the use of pesticides, and reduction in biogenetic diversity. The tendency toward monoculture—single-crop farming—aggravated all of these adverse effects. Monoculture and plant diversity are discussed again in my chapter on "Place-Based Education." For now it is enough to note that monoculture, while efficient in producing high yields, increases the vulnerability of crops to highly specialized insect pests and plant diseases. That vulnerability leads to heavy use of pesticides and damage to helpful insects, other plant species, and both soil and water.

The examples discussed here—and many more could be offered—illustrate the need for knowledge. Knowledge, as noted earlier, is not by itself sufficient; it can be used in behalf of global concerns or of self-interest. Global citizens need commitment to well-informed choices, and they must be motivated by global concerns. Young people are often idealistic, and they can be recruited to movements advertising high ideals. Their very immaturity, as John Dewey said, implies the capacity for growth and helps us to believe in "the possibilities of a better life for the community as well as for individuals" (1930, 99). But immaturity and the impulses that accompany it must be guided by knowledge. Teachers must promote information-gathering, reflection, and critical thinking. It is not enough to adopt the right slogans; we must know what we are doing.

Secondary school teachers of the social studies and related subjects should survey available texts with a critical eye. In an age when the emphasis on historical facts is increasing, where will students encounter the topics central to any attempt to develop sustainable ways of life? Do the texts discuss water resources and political battles over water? Do they present the benefits and harms of large dams? Do they discuss the benefits of plant diversity? Do they help students to understand the deep love people of widely varying cultures express for their home places? Do any of the texts urge students to develop an understanding and appreciation of their own home places? It would be instructive for curriculum groups to compare the indexes of standard American history texts with that of Steinberg's *Down to Earth*, subtitled *Nature's Role in American History*. Do the standard texts omit much of the knowledge students need to become global citizens?

Contemporary concern for the health of the whole Earth as an ecosystem can be traced to the work of Rachel Carson (1962). Although ecology was not a new idea, Carson gave it new vigor. The basic idea of ecology is interdependence, and that is also a basic concept in global citizenship. Before we intervene drastically in environmental relations, we should know what these relations are and what the likely effects of our intervention might be. Carson helped us to understand that the use of certain pesticides not only destroys harmful insects but also sometimes eliminates the insects on which birds depend for their food. Further, the poison used to protect plants works its way through the food chain to harm creatures we do not intend to hurt.

Applied on a global level, ecological thinking brings us to consider the effects of life in one locality on the lives and well-being of distant others. Several international meetings of scientists have ended in agreements that reflect global thinking. Edward O. Wilson summarizes the scientific recommendations of the last two decades on the preservation of endangered species of plants and animals (Wilson 2002, 160–164). His summary includes the protection of the world's "hot spots"—those habitats that are both at the greatest risk and shelter the largest concentration of species found nowhere else on earth (Wilson 2002, 160). People must be well educated to understand that the destruction of ecosystems in Ecuador and the Philippines affects all of us and, especially, the quality of life for future generations.

In addition to acting now to save endangered species, global citizens must be concerned about the Earth's air, water, and climate. Every industrial nation in the world except the United States has promised to ratify the Kyoto Protocol, which limits the carbon emissions that produce the greenhouse effect. The United States is the world's greatest offender, and yet it has protested that it should not have to cut back on carbon emissions unless the underdeveloped nations are also compelled to do so! Singer quotes figures showing that "the United States, with about 5 percent of the world's population, was responsible for 30 percent of the cumulative emissions" (Singer 2002, 32). American students will have to accept some hard facts about their own nation in order to become global citizens.

But students should also be encouraged to find positive programs in the United States. Massive tree-planting programs have been launched, for example, and much of the East Coast, once denuded of trees, has been reforested. Further, the program of tree planting has become a national ecological commitment. Should the United States be forgiven for its unhealthy level of carbon emissions because it plants so many trees to soak up the carbon dioxide? Michael Pollan suggests that we should "think of the tree as Earth's breathing apparatus, an organ that helps regulate the planet's atmosphere by exhaling fresh oxygen and inhaling the carbon that animals, decay, and civilization spew into it" (1991, 205), but he does not argue that planting trees eliminates the need to reduce carbon emissions, and most scientists agree that, praiseworthy as tree planting surely is, emissions must be cut.

In concluding this section, I ask readers to consider Wilson's summary:

> A sense of genetic unity, kinship, and deep history are among the values that bond us to the living environment. They are survival mechanisms for ourselves and our species. To conserve biological diversity is an investment in immortality. (2002, 133)

In the biological world, diversity supports unity; there can be no whole without diversity. Can the same be said about cultural diversity? We turn to that question next.

SOCIAL AND CULTURAL DIVERSITY

Diversity in the social world is different from diversity in the biological world. We human beings all belong to the same species; the value of social diversity is not a matter of interdependence among different species. One could even argue (and some have) that the health and stability of the social world might be better served by a reduction in diversity. Yet *diversity* has become a buzzword in today's political/social interactions, and it takes considerable courage to raise questions about the concept. In a later chapter, Robert Nash reminds us that *diversity* refers merely to difference. If we want to claim something of value for diversity, we have to say what that something is and why it should be valued.

Let's start by asking what sort of diversity we want to preserve. Then we can ask why we should preserve the types we've identified and what this preservation has to do with global citizenship. We can eliminate some forms of diversity immediately—pernicious differences in economic well-being, differences in health and physical soundness, and differences in rights and liberties defined by gender or social or religious class. If we could, we would also eliminate the drastic differences in moral capacities exemplified in various psychosocial pathologies. Few would argue that the presence of lepers, hunchbacks, beggars, untouchables, robbers, and psychopaths adds to a rich diversity that should be valued and preserved. Insofar as it is in the power of caring citizens, we would like to prevent or cure disease and handicaps, remove discrimination, eliminate poverty, and find a cure for moral incompetence.

Diversity, as we refer to it today, usually involves racial, ethnic, and religious differences, and when we use the word, we point to a desirable mix of people representing these differences. *Diversity* is used as a reason for engaging in forms of affirmative action, and those who oppose such action are often thought to be unenlightened or even bigoted. As educators, however, we would do well to raise questions so that the positions we take will be well-reasoned and not simply ideological reactions.

What is valuable about racial or ethnic diversity? Would the world be worse off if we all had nearly the same skin color, hair texture, body build, and eye shape? On the one hand, many of us feel that race shouldn't enter politics and policymaking at all, and some scientists have even argued that there is no persuasive scientific basis for the concept of race. On the other hand, race clearly does matter in most societies, and the race someone is born into has a significant impact on his or her life experience. It is this difference in life experience to which we usually refer when arguing the benefits of diversity. But which of the differences in life experience should we treasure and preserve? Which do we want to eliminate, and when we have eliminated the undesirable differences, on what basis will we argue (if we continue to do so) for diversity?

One answer to this question (which we can only begin to consider here) is that a heritage will remain. Human survival may not depend on the preservation of racial/cultural heritages, but human life is certainly enriched by the existence of different cultural practices, and cultural practices are influenced by race.

Another answer pushes us to reconsider the value of physical characteristics as valuable contributions to diversity. Certainly we do not want to maintain disabilities and any differences that prevent people from participating fully in social life. It may be, however, that studying and working with people of different colors and physical capacities actually makes unity more likely. To ensure that racial discrimination does not arise anew (after we have

eliminated it), it may be wise to provide students and workers with continued opportunities to see that these surface differences are rarely relevant to
the tasks at hand. It may even be that the participation of obviously black
African-Americans promotes the goal of unity more effectively than that of
lighter-skinned members of the race who share the same heritage. Now, am
I suggesting that people should get "more points" for having darker (or more
obviously different) skin color? Of course not. I am suggesting something
that we often overlook—that diversity based on "mere" physical, observable differences among people may act to deter the virus of prejudice and
bigotry. This kind of diversity may be thought of as analogous to plant di-
versification. Just as monoculture in agriculture invites the attack of specialized pests and diseases, separation and isolation of people by observable
differences irrelevant to the activities in which they engage may invite stereotyping and other forms of prejudice.

   We have not yet come to grips with what is perhaps the most important
reason for recognizing and appreciating diversity. This reason is that differences exist. So long as differences exist and are considered important, ignoring them is equivalent to not listening—hence to not caring. Where people
not only claim difference but also celebrate it, global citizens cannot pretend that differences are unimportant. Diversity becomes essential in all
policymaking conversations, because we must hear the voice of the other.
Jacques Derrida (1978) tells us that we must learn to let the other be *as other*;
that is, we should not assume that others are just like us, nor should we force
them to be so. We heard this message from Stiglitz and Berlin earlier. Our
shield against such an assumption and the coercion that follows it is an invited and valued diversity of equal participants.

   There is, then, a sense in which diversity, or better, *pluralism* (as Nash
argues), plays a role in human survival. Because diversity exists, pluralism—
sharing power with all those affected by policies and decisions—is necessary
for human survival. We have for too long killed and mistreated one another
over racial, ethnic, and religious differences.

   Religious differences are among the most troubling and have caused
untold suffering. Nash argues strongly that educators must find ways to
promote both tolerance and understanding. I agree with him that we must
try, but the task is a difficult one. So far we have not even found ways in
which to discuss religious questions at the precollege level (Noddings 1993),
and most of us are acutely uncomfortable in talking about religion with others who may not share our beliefs. Indeed, as Nash points out, many believers know little about the formal doctrines and histories of their own religions.

   It is not enough to say that everyone has the right to practice his or her
own religion without interference. As I asked earlier, if a religion discrimi-
nates against women, should we tolerate that discrimination? Does it matter whether the discrimination occurs within our national boundaries or

somewhere else in the world? If it does, have we met another obstacle to global citizenship?

When we look at the woes and troubles created by differences in the world, it is not surprising that many people prefer an emphasis on unity rather than difference. One difficulty with unity as a goal is that it has long been associated with nationalism or loyalty to some particular group. At what level should we seek unity? Or should we seek it for limited purposes in different places?

Arthur Schlesinger Jr. incurred the wrath of many fellow liberals when he seemed to attack the multiculturalism advocated by current liberalism. It is worth looking carefully at what he said and why it induced such anger. In one of his sharpest paragraphs, he wrote:

> The militants of ethnicity now contend that a main objective of public education should be the protection, celebration, and perpetuation of ethnic origins and identities. Separation, however, nourishes prejudices, magnifies differences, and stirs antagonisms. The consequent increase in ethnic and racial conflict lies behind the hullabaloo over "multiculturalism" and "political correctness," over the iniquities of the "Eurocentric" curriculum, and over the notion that history and literature should be taught not as intellectual disciplines but as therapies whose function is to raise minority self-esteem. (1992, 17)

Schlesinger contrasts this new ethnic militancy with an earlier attitude that sought and celebrated, first, the creation of a unique American identity and, later, assimilation of newcomers to that identity. The idea that people should cling to previous identities while claiming American citizenship shocks Schlesinger. He is probably right in pointing out that separatism may increase prejudices and antagonisms. I have already suggested as much. However, he may be wrong in saying that group identity "nourishes" those prejudices and "magnifies" differences. It may simply make them visible, drawing attention to what has previously been suffered in silence. Further, when he suggests that history and literature should be taught as "intellectual disciplines," he seems to forget who defined these disciplines and whose self-esteem was promoted (even if implicitly) by their dominance in the curriculum.

There is much to deplore in this paragraph, but the basic worry expressed—that we are losing the *unum* in *e pluribus unum*—is an important worry. The question for present purposes is where that *unum* should be located. Should our efforts go toward the revival of national unity or toward the new and fragile notion of global unity? If it is national unity that concerns us, there is a solution that has almost always worked—war. Sadly, with rare exceptions, war brings us together as a nation and gives meaning to individual lives (Hedges 2002). Is there no other way to find unity across differences? Will it take an invasion of aliens from outer space to unite Earth's people?

Liberal advocates of multiculturalism see great strength in the movement that so troubles Schlesinger. The purpose of multicultural curricula is not therapeutic, as Schlesinger fears (although the therapeutic function is not all bad) but, as Rob Reich describes it "*civic*—it is in the interests of all citizens" (2002, 140), and this is why such curricula should interest global citizens. The purpose of attending to differences, including them in our curricula and celebrating them, is to establish formerly neglected groups as full citizens—people who are heard and recognized. The same purpose should guide our commitment to global citizenship. We should not need a common enemy to draw us together. As we have seen, diversity, pluralism, and multiculturalism—rightly understood—protect us from our worst social/political impulses.

We have not yet discussed intellectual diversity—differences expressed in opinions, political attitudes, and arguments. This form of diversity is said to be highly valued in academic and political circles. In principle, it is valued, but in practice the pressure is all too often toward conformity. In academe the range of difference is limited by the criteria that define disciplines and professional practices; within each of these, further criteria separate the acceptable from the unacceptable. In politics, unity is sought at the party level, and it is hard to transcend party lines and keep one's place in political life. In both academe and politics, there is an inclination to join a side (party or school of thought) and use its language as a sign of one's bona fides. Instead of thinking through an issue (as we've tried to do here all too briefly), the temptation is to ask, What does my group think on this? What shall I say as a faithful representative of my group? The worst features of political correctness are captured in these questions.

Critical thinking must be prepared to jump across established lines, and thinkers who dare to question the opinions of their own groups should not be cast out or ostracized. As Dewey and others have advised, societies should cherish their dissenters because they may remind us of our fallibility and point us toward new possibilities. When dissent is extreme, we are faced with a new problem: are we listening to a prophet or a crackpot? We have to listen, engage in dialogue, reflect, and make a commitment.

Another form of diversity to be cherished is that of talents and interests. Here again, most people agree in principle, but our practice is schizophrenic. On the one hand, we value plumbers and carpenters (we *need* them); on the other, our educational system devalues the children who will be our future plumbers and carpenters and urges them to "do better." Equality of opportunity is construed as giving everyone a fair chance to do what only a privileged few have done in the past. The generous arrogance that we met earlier in other settings shows itself again. I am not suggesting that children should be sorted into occupational ways of life at an early age; educators should not engage in sorting. I am recommending that all human talents be recognized and nourished so that students can make well-informed choices (Noddings 2003a). At the present time, instead of helping all children to become competent and happy in work chosen to fit their talents, we insist that they all be measured by the same yardstick. Then they are sorted by that uniform measure, and young people who might have chosen an occupation proudly find themselves in it by default because they were "not good enough" to meet the uniform expectations of a society unwilling to examine its own values.

The survival of postindustrial societies really does depend on this last form of diversity. The world as we know it would quickly fall apart if everyone spent her days as I do (or as any other individual does). We need one another, and that truth should be recognized and celebrated in schools.

EDUCATING FOR PEACE

Peace and global citizenship are entwined. I suggested earlier that peace may be a precondition for global citizenship, but teaching for global citizenship may also help to promote peace. It is not easy, however, to teach for global citizenship when war threatens. Not only may teachers feel pressed to omit important topics, but they may also allow some views to be distorted in order to preserve the spirit of national citizenship. All sorts of questionable slogans and verbal justifications become familiar, and anyone who challenges them may be labeled unpatriotic. World War I, for example, was promoted as the war "to make the world safe for democracy," and those who actively opposed it were ridiculed, harassed, and sometimes imprisoned. After the destruction of the Twin Towers on September 11, 2001, writers who suggested that the United States should consider why it was incurring such hatred were accused of trying to justify terrorism. Early in 2003, we were told that war with Iraq must be undertaken in order to preserve the world's peace. Those who find such language Orwellian are once again castigated as disloyal, unwilling to face the facts, and even as "left loonies."

Understandably, teachers may find it easier to talk about the need to establish a democracy in Iraq than about the presumed sanctity of national borders and global agreements against preemptive wars. Similarly, it will be easier to emphasize the promise of leaders to spare as many innocent lives as possible than to talk frankly about the number of Iraqi lives lost in the Gulf War and its aftermath. Where can students find these figures, and why are they so rarely publicized? Educating for global citizenship requires us to value the lives of all people, not just those of our own nation. Students should be made aware that this ideal is always lost in all-out war.

With this very brief discussion of the atmosphere in early 2003, we can see that educating for peace and global citizenship, always a fragile enterprise, is again at risk. There is no shortage of material to draw upon for peace education, and there are hundreds of organizations devoted to the promotion of peace (Harris and Morrison 2003; Stein 1993). Why, then, have we made so little progress in establishing peace studies as an essential part of the school curriculum?

It is not only that the times dictate the emphasis in school studies. Almost certainly 2003 was a time in which American strength, virtue, heroism, and ideals were emphasized. But there are related problems that transcend the events of a particular time. Two important ones should be mentioned: first, political history has long concentrated on wars and the rise and fall of nations; second, the school curriculum is still organized around traditional disciplines. Peace educators are thus faced with the difficult question of where peace studies should be located in the curriculum.

Assuming that the present organization around the disciplines will not change in the near future, we have to consider what can be done within those subjects. Let's look first at history. I have a popular high school American history textbook in front of me. Its index contains no entry for "*peace*." (It does have one for "Peace Corps.") It does, of course, discuss the termination of various wars, and it mentions that Jane Addams and Theodore Roosevelt were awarded the Nobel Peace prize, but there is no organized discussion of the prize. The two mentions appear separately and incidentally. Similarly, resistance to war and dedicated effort toward meaningful peace are scattered here and there in the text. *War*, not *peace*, is the organizing concept.

What should be included in the history curriculum if we are serious about educating for peace? It seems reasonable to say that there should be a comprehensive discussion of movements for peace and nonviolence, and the material should be drawn from events and literature worldwide. But immediately a worry arises about how much of this can be done in *history*. In his account of the tradition of nonviolence, Michael True (1995) discusses literature, art, music, labor movements, and religion. Should the ballads of Woody Guthrie, Pete Seeger, and Joan Baez be part of the history curriculum? Peace educators might say an enthusiastic yes to this. Should Thoreau's essay on civil disobedience be part of the social studies curriculum, or does it belong (if at all) in the English curriculum? The concern here is that topics on nonviolence will be so scattered, if they are introduced at all, that students will not acquire a sense of coherence and movement in the tradition. It would be good, of course, to have topics on peace appear in all subjects, but they should not be avoided when they arise in one subject simply because they "belong" in another.

We might also suggest that attention be given to women's resistance to war (Reardon 1985; Ruddick 1989). In treating this topic, we should be careful to point out that women have not always resisted war. On the contrary, they have often backed war enthusiastically and rejected men who refused to participate in it (Elshtain 1987; Ruddick 1989). Still, there is an important contribution to be considered, and heroic tales to be told. For example, Jane Addams risked her reputation opposing World War I, and Jeannette Rankin sacrificed her political career by voting in Congress against both world wars. Just recently, Barbara Lee cast the sole vote against unlimited use of military force in the fight against terrorism. (See the account at www.brc21.org.)

The solidarity of women's efforts for peace is lost if comments on it are thrown about loosely in histories organized around war. Feminists have made a related contribution to nonviolence in their insistence on *peace* as more than a cessation of war. So long as groups of people of one gender are victims of violence or live in fear of violence, there is no real peace (Buchwald, Fletcher, and Roth 1993). This observation suggests the need to include material on the oppression of women, racial minorities, homosexuals, and various religious sects in any adequate curriculum for peace education.

Peace movements sponsored by religions should also be included in the history curriculum. In trying to do this, we encounter a triple difficulty. As Nash points out in his chapter, many public school teachers are afraid to address religious topics at all. Second, these topics rarely appear in widely used textbooks. Third, as we have already noted, peace is almost never used as an organizing theme in the history curriculum. Still, for energetic and courageous teachers, materials are available (Smith-Christopher 2000). It is especially important today, when religion is so frequently associated with conflict and terror (Juergensmeyer 2000), for students to be aware of religious efforts to establish peace.

Our efforts at peace education should not, however, be restricted to history. Many thinkers have suggested that literature and the visual arts can be powerful in both peace education and moral education. Virginia Woolf (1966) argued that a comparative study of the world's literature, painting, and music should work against nationalistic emotions and patriotism. Identifying herself as an outsider (because women at that time had not attained equality with men), she wrote: "In fact, as a woman, I have no country. As a woman I want no country. As a woman my country is the whole world" (1966, 109). Then noting that she might yet be moved by love for the natural beauty of England, she suggested that "this drop of pure, if irrational, emotion she [the outsider] will make serve her to give England first what she desires of peace and freedom for the whole world" (p. 109). She thus urges us to convert patriotism to a gentle love that will spread over our own land and hence to the larger world. Surely this is a patriotism that peace educators can endorse.

Susan Sontag (2002, 2003), building on Woolf's work, explores the possibility that visual images might so frighten and disgust us that we would give up war. But then she reminds us that images of horrors have long been with us, and have not turned men away from fighting. Her essay is a cogent reminder that we have not yet found an educational medium that will dependably inoculate us against war. Indeed, images that disgust some of us and turn us toward pacifism seem to excite others and make them eager to be part of great battles (Juergensmeyer 2000). It is reasonable, however, to include both literature and art in our curriculum for peace. If they provide no guarantee, they do offer rich possibilities. Those possibilities include discussion on the differential effects of viewing images of destruction.

What can be done in science education to contribute to peace? Science educators today are concerned with ecological issues, and war violently disrupts the world's ecology. Every conscientious science teacher dedicated to peace should plan to go outside his or her discipline to find material that is relevant to both science and peace education. Many accounts of wartime environmental destruction are available. From the poisonous defoliation employed in Vietnam to the widespread destruction of the natural environment caused by the building of airstrips and military roads in the South Pacific during World War II (Schrijvers 2002), military history reveals a pattern of ecological disaster.

Math teachers can ask students to trace the figures on casualties for 20th-century wars. The numbers are horrifying, and the shift from military to civilian casualties is alarming. Wars are no longer fought by soldiers against soldiers. Noncombatants are the main victims of today's warfare. Some years ago in a calculus class I taught, students were working on equations associated with radioactive decay. They began to talk about the atomic bombing of Hiroshima and Nagasaki. There were arguments about the justification of such bombing. One student summed up what seemed to be the class's consensus: no nation or group should use weapons that kill so many people. I nodded in agreement, but then I asked, How many is it all right to kill? Silence followed. I think many of the students began to see that humankind must seek alternatives to war if we are to survive. Opportunities to discuss such issues arise in every school subject, but teachers often fail to use them. Katherine Simon (2001) has shown how often moral questions arise in classrooms only to be ignored by teachers afraid to handle them—even in literature classes.

The secondary curriculum should also include a full discussion of the personal risks, horrors, and losses of war. Young people who may serve in the armed forces should understand not only what may happen to them but also what they might do to others. Warriors risk losing their moral resources (Glover 2000), and for some this loss is worse than death. Many writers have documented the moral perversion that accompanies war (Glover 2000; James 1929; Walzer 1977). Young men who would never have hurt their neighbors commit atrocious acts in war, and as a result some of them never recover full mental and emotional health. When we think of education as preparation for adult life, we must consider disclosure of what students may face in serving their country. The aim here is not to disillusion students with stories of the atrocities committed by "our" soldiers; every army commits atrocious acts. The aim is to give students an honest account that may help them to preserve their moral integrity or, at least, to understand how it may be lost.

In the following chapters, writers suggest answers to some of the questions I've raised here, and they present readers with some further issues. My chapter starts with a discussion of place-based education, arguing that a global view is hard to develop without a sound understanding of one's local environment and the real love that many human beings have for their home regions. In her chapter, Gloria Ladson-Billings reminds us that U.S. schools provide educators with a microcosm of problems inherent in the idea of global citizenship. By practicing inclusion and respect in our schools, we set the stage for practical consideration of global citizenship. Stephen Thornton also discusses the many obstacles we face in educating for global citizenship, but he argues that including internationalism in the current social studies curriculum will both advance a global perspective and enrich existing courses. He also shows how nationalism and internationalism are inextricably related in the modern world. In all three chapters, we see an emphasis on the connection between local and global arenas.

Gender and religion are clearly important topics to be treated in a global curriculum. Peggy McIntosh argues that the caregiving tasks traditionally associated with women and so little valued by political leaders are actually fundamental in developing an environment of global cooperation. Similarly, Robert Nash advises teachers to help students listen to one another attentively and respectfully as they discuss issues of religion. Like Ladson-Billings, they emphasize inclusion in attitudes, knowledge, and cooperative activity.

Nancy Carlsson-Paige and Linda Lantieri show us how middle-school students develop a sense of social justice and apply it in both local and global situations. Readers will be impressed by what these youngsters learn and what they accomplish in real settings. Also working directly with young students, Stacie Nicole Smith and David Fairman echo Thornton's call for curriculum integration, and they show—with many convincing examples—how students can learn and exercise skills associated with conflict resolution.

In the concluding chapter, I make an attempt to evaluate how well we have done in addressing the issues raised in this Introduction and to summarize the tasks that face us as global educators.

CHAPTER 1

Gender Perspectives on Educating for Global Citizenship

Peggy McIntosh

THIS CHAPTER EXPLORES WAYS in which concepts of citizenship can be expanded to encompass affective dimensions, including habits of mind, heart, body, and soul. Underlying this approach to citizenship is the value of working for and preserving a network of relationship and connection across lines of difference and distinctness, while keeping and deepening a sense of one's own identity and integrity. In this work, there is much to learn from gender studies and personal experience, both of which are explored here.

DEFINING GLOBAL CITIZENSHIP

The 21st century requires us to think about citizenship as extending far beyond the "city" from which the word derives, and the state and the nation with which it has also been associated. Throughout the history of the United States, the matter of what citizenship entails has been contested. But a citizen is generally defined as a person having duties, rights, responsibilities, and privileges within a political unit that demands loyalty from that person and extends protection in return. Since we are living on a shrinking planet and are made contiguous with others by technology, commerce, conflicts, international networks, and the environment, the question arises of how citizenship could be redefined if one of its dimensions were felt membership in a political and social unit that is the whole globe.

The very definitions of citizenship need to be changed before the political and social unit can be conceived of as the globe itself. Political definitions of citizenship would need to be augmented by more affective definitions. The ideas of loyalty, protection, duties, rights, responsibilities, and privileges would need to be expanded and multiplied to the point where one's loyalty and expectation of protection come not only from such units as the living place, province, or nation, but also from a sense of belonging to the whole world. Within this vast world, the marks of citizenship would need to include affection, respect, care, curiosity, and concern for the well-being of all living beings.

What would it take to be global citizens? I can answer only from my own experience and perceptions. I associate the idea of a global citizen with habits of mind, heart, body, and soul that have to do with working for and preserving a network of relationship and connection across lines of difference and distinctness, while keeping and deepening a sense of one's own identity and integrity.

I associate global citizenship first with several capacities of mind: 1) the ability to observe oneself and the world around one, 2) the ability to make comparisons and contrasts, 3) the ability to "see" plurally as a result, 4) the ability to understand that both "reality" and language come in versions, 5) the ability to see power relations and understand them systemically, and 6) the ability to balance awareness of one's own realities with the realities of entities outside of the perceived self. These capacities of mind may be developed through daily life anywhere and fostered in many ways. They do not require literacy. But in our technologically interconnected world—and through experience in reading, writing, imagining, and traveling—such mind capacities can become well developed. They do not fit well with the world of formal education as it is carried on in the United States. But for me, they are key constituents of global awareness and they point toward values of transglobal communication and peaceful coexistence.

I also associate global citizenship with several capacities of heart: 1) the ability to respect one's own feelings and delve deeply into them, 2) the ability to become aware of others' feelings and to believe in the validity of those feelings, 3) the ability to experience in oneself a mixture of conflicting feelings without losing a sense of integrity, 4) the ability to experience affective worlds plurally while keeping a gyroscopic sense of one's core orientations, 5) the capacity to wish competing parties well, 6) the ability to observe and understand how the "politics of location" affect one's own and others' positions and power in the world, and 7) the ability to balance being heartfelt with a felt knowledge of how culture is embedded in the hearts of ourselves and others. These heart capacities can, I believe, be strong in many people who are not literate, and I observe that they are often quite weak in people who have a great deal of formal education. It is as though strengthening the muscles that allow one to compete in the economic realms of the capitalist world weakens the muscles needed for entertaining multiple emotional connections balancing many complexities of life.

I further associate global citizenship with related capacities of the physical body and the spiritual soul. The global citizen knows his or her body not as a tool for mastery or beauty, but as a body in the body of the world. We have both unique individuality and intricate, inevitable connection with other bodies in the local and global habitats we share. Knowledge of self and other, comparison and contrast between the self and others, plural understanding of the integrity of all beings, and a sense of balance between dependence and interdependence in the physical world are all elements in the development of a global citizen's sense of inhabiting and using a body. Knowledge of our mortality, knowledge that being born entails dying, is part of the wisdom of the body. Respect for our own and others' physical needs is part of the wisdom of the body.

I feel that the soul needs a certain sweetness to be that of a global citizen. Observing turbulence and stillness, comparing and contrasting the outcomes of various kinds of human desire and behavior, I think that the global soul seeks the nondestructive as it seeks to preserve the bodies that house souls. Yet I also see souls of global citizens taking part in the dangerous conflicts of the contentious world, engaging rather than withdrawing, in order that the personality may be put in the service of something larger than itself, and that danger and suffering may be alleviated.

What I have sketched here goes beyond most discussions of citizenship and bears the strong marks of my own experience working with women and doing research on gender relations. It seems to me that many of the qualities that I am defining as essential to global citizenship are qualities that are gender-related. That is, they have been especially delegated to, conditioned in, and rewarded in women. When females bring forth children or do the caretaking that is expected of us, we are automatically placed in obvious relation to other beings and must develop many capacities for plural seeing and feeling: capacities for comparison and contrast, hearing more than one voice, understanding more than one version of self-interest, being empathic persons who have the capacity to hold and to internalize, as our own, more than one version of reality. Women have been charged with caring about the decent survival of all. This charge deeply affects our development.

I do not know, and other researchers do not know, the extent to which these capacities in women are biologically based, and it is very hard to find this out through empirical research. Some must be, in part, biologically based. But if we observe changes over the last century in women's and men's lives in the industrialized world, it is possible to conclude that many forms of gender socialization in the past were based on invented notions of what is appropriate to males and females. Experimentation has shown that these notions can change. Only continuing experimentation can tell us now what the actual limits of male and female capacity are. I do not feel that the capacities for global citizenship and plural competency that I am describing are the purview of women alone, or that they should be. In U.S. society, this openness is, for example, common in small boys before the society delivers messages to them such as "boys don't cry," which weakens their sense of self-knowledge and undermines their ability to feel empathy or acknowledge vulnerability.

In any case, women's ascribed roles in all societies especially require attentiveness to others, and the capacity to hear and take in many voices, stories, and versions simultaneously. Without these capacities women cannot do well the tasks of caretaking they have been assigned. They entail what Jean Baker Miller terms "the emotional housekeeping of the world," and they are crucial to human survival (Miller 1976).

I believe that the transpersonal care and understanding that women have been asked to do is central to history and to citizenship. It is not, however, central to the discussion of citizenship that focuses on rights, responsibilities, and public duties. Insofar as the public world has been assigned to men, as men's definitions of what citizenship is about have prevailed in its definitions. Within patriarchy, male definitions of reality trump female experience. Behind the scenes of what is presented to us as "history," women make and mend the fabric of society. "Lower-caste" men are likewise expected to make and mend the fabric. Those who wield the most public power are seen to be the leaders of citizens, but in fact the alternative fabric of day-by-day maintenance of citizens exists in a world more or less out of sight of public discussion. This lateral work requires a patience and sensibility focused on "getting through" and "getting on," rather than "getting ahead." The nurturance of each generation depends on this lateral, ongoing way of sustaining life in the world.

EDUCATING GLOBAL CITIZENS

I feel that in order to educate global citizens, we need to give young people in school training and support in the little-named skills of what Miller once called, in an unpublished talk, "finding one's development through the development of others," that is, the skills of working for, and wanting, the commonweal, the well-being of all. Young people need rewards for and experiences of caring as a vital part of citizenship and a vital aspect of themselves. In other words, they all need to respect and develop qualities in themselves and in the culture as a whole that were conditioned into women or lower-caste men, who were expected to make and mend the fabric of the society behind the scenes. For the whole point of making and mending the fabric is to keep the self and the habitat, social or ecological, alive and whole.

When the emphasis is put on making and mending the social fabric as a central value for all citizens, then the emphasis can shift, as I feel it should, away from "rights" to "needs" as the basis for local and global policy and care. I feel that "rights" are an invention by 18th-century European thinkers and are not biologically demonstrable. The hand of the Creator did not descend and present us with rights. Human needs, on the other hand, are empirically verifiable and are in all of us. Water, food, clothing, shelter, and meaningful connection with other human beings are basic needs without whose fulfillment we die. The ethos of global citizenship, I believe, must start with providing, and caring about providing, these basic human necessities, and the protections for the sustaining ecosystems that humans depend on.

Can U.S. educators muster the character needed to widen the sense of loyalty and care in themselves and in students beyond the units of family, team, class, school, town, city, state, and nation? At present, most teachers and their students have not been educated to think that good character might require thinking or feeling so broadly or plurally. For most, the United States as a nation is the outermost ring of the series of concentric loyalties suggested above. Beyond this national margin are other peoples and nations mostly seen as competitors, threats, or unknowns, none of them measuring up to the United States. Technology, however, insistently reminds us of our commonalities with others beyond our borders. The national values have not yet caught up.

Another obstruction to bringing what I see as empathetic and plural-minded global citizenship into education is that many educators and parents today in the United States would see compassionate values as undermining the society by undermining the innate nature of boys and men. A myth persists that male and female are "opposite" sexes, and a patriarchal conviction persists that male and female are not equally valuable. In fact, the sexes overlap; in many ways men and women are similar physiologically and psychologically. Either sex can be shown to demonstrate an edge in ability and capacity. Nevertheless, the myths of oppositeness and of male superiority require that males be protected from developing attributes that have been projected onto women. These attributes are seen to undermine, and even to contaminate, masculinity. Males, especially young males, may have strong competencies in the caring, the relationality, and the plural seeing that I think are essential for global citizenship. What is rewarded in them, however, is solo risk-taking and individualism, and if they are white males, a go-it-alone and "damn-the-torpedoes" kind of bravery without a balanced regard for, or awareness of, the outcomes for other people of one's behaviors. Resistance against the kind of global education that I favor is to be expected in the United States in this day and age, since it seems to undermine the values of white male individualism. I favor, however, a balance in all citizens between virtues that have been projected differentially onto people of different groups, on the theory that all of our human virtues carry some validity, and that relational aspects of our personalities are needed in everyone because our world needs plural-minded citizens with capacities for concern and compassion in every citizen.

GENDER ROLES AND GLOBAL EDUCATION

It is my opinion that both men and women hold within them the capacities that have been projected onto those of the "opposite sex," or "opposite" races or ethnic groups. These capacities in and of themselves are neither negative nor positive. For example, in terms of gender among white people in the United States, individuation and bravery are important human qualities that both sexes would do well to cultivate, as both may be needed at some time in one's life and in the life of one's community. But patriarchy and white supremacy are strong societal frameworks in the United States. Each keeps rules, perceptions, standards, definitions, and control in the hands of a dominant group. Whether or not the members of the dominant group are nice people has no bearing on these dynamics. Within patriarchy, white supremacy, or any other hierarchical system, a power imbalance is inevitable; the attributes projected onto and rewarded in the dominant group count for more than the attributes projected onto and rewarded in members of a subordinate group. Roles projected onto and expected of women—like being attentive to and protective of vulnerable things—are not valued alongside of valor and acquisition of power for the self, as projected onto men, especially white men, in the United States. Cultural restrictions on developing into "whole" persons interfere with the development of global citizens who have individual integrity as well as cosmopolitan attentiveness to the existence and well-being of others. This balance, though I see it as wholeness, would be seen by many as "not strong enough, not male enough" within a U.S. context. So I see a need within school curricula to explore strength and courage more broadly and deeply, to offset the individualistic presentation of heroism, as it is frequently studied in our schools, with the study of goodness and strength in making and mending the fabrics of culture.

A related difficulty in educating global citizens in the United States may reside in the tepid response of many Americans to the idea of citizenship itself. The concept of leadership has had more appeal, as something muscular, tough, interesting, stimulating, and rewarding. And although patriotism has been a very strong emotion in the nation since September 11, 2001, I think that citizenship still has less appeal, being associated with obligations, docility, obedience, and good behavior. It could be that in the popular white mind, citizenship is to women as leadership is to men. Citizenship is not necessarily heroic, expressive, or creative. It is seen as involving responsibilities, duties, and what must be done without the status of social reward. Leadership is seen to enable individuality and special status, whereas citizenship is seen as a social leveler. The United States government prides itself on global leadership, on being out in front as the sole superpower. But in my view, as the 21st century begins, the administration of George W. Bush shows no capacity for, nor understanding of, global citizenship; that is, of belonging within an entity larger than the nation itself. It is hard to press for education of global citizens in a nation whose government is acting out the role of the independent, dominant, unapproachable, individualistic, lone power whose self-interest is seen as the ethos that should prevail throughout the world.

Despite the dominant cultural values of U.S. society and education, many valiant teachers have construed education more broadly and have attempted to do global teaching in the light of their own understandings of intelligence, growth, and development for their students. I received some formal global schooling myself in the 1950s that is illuminating for me to think back on now. Remembering both its content and my resistance to the content sheds light on dynamics that I believe persist in the minds and hearts of many white U.S. citizens. This global education occurred because my parents were appalled when the United States dropped the atomic bombs on Hiroshima and Nagasaki in 1945. They became Quakers and pacifists and transferred me to a Quaker school when I was 15 years old. I thought that the plural and gender-fair education I received there was annoying and ridiculous. For example, I had a weird teacher by the name of Mr. Cleveland who taught World Religions, with an "s." It seemed to me that Mr. Cleveland wasted our time. He taught about Buddhism, Hinduism, Islam, Taoism, and Confucianism. I was in school to learn about "the best." I felt that he diluted the class with extraneous books and people. I was filled with scorn when he said there were many paths up the mountain of religious belief. I felt he should take an interest only in "the right path."

Having inflicted comparative religions on us, i.e., comparative "seeing" of a kind that I now believe that global citizens need, Mr. Cleveland went on to teach Semantics, which I also resisted intellectually and emotionally. In fairness, I should empathize with the self I was in those days. World War II had just ended, a war that may be considered a simpler war, morally, for the United States than any subsequent war we have been involved in. I was in a bipolar mode of thinking: win/lose, right/wrong. Mr. Cleveland complexified all that simplicity with the study of semantics. It upset me to be told that "what I say" may not be "what you hear." I believed there was or should be a direct transfer from one mind to another, and that given two different interpretations of what had been said, only one of the two could be right. And if we were right in World War II and the Germans and Japanese were wrong, why on earth did this teacher and his colleagues at my new school hold work camps in Germany and invite Japanese students to attend the school?

Another problem with Mr. Cleveland was that he introduced us to Theories of History. I wanted to hear only one theory, which went approximately this way: People encounter problems in their climb toward perfection. Wars and depressions are such problems, or setbacks. We are now in a post-Depression and postwar time and are making progress toward the millennium, when history will be further along toward perfection. Mr. Cleveland, however, gave us bizarre alternative versions: pendulum theories, spiral theories, progress theories, and descent theories. He said we could think about history as "coming down through the ages" or "coming up through the ages," and that each was a different conceptualization and that the differences were interesting. I was so impatient with this man's attention to differences!

The crowning stupidity, I thought, came when our class put on a play and instead of directing it himself, as head of the Drama Department, he appointed a student director. Though I was the student director, I thought this was a result of the fact that Mr. Cleveland simply didn't know what he was doing. John Dewey might have given several years of his life to know that teachers would actually do this kind of teaching in which students' growth and development are placed at the center of instruction. And I am now aware that his decision to empower a girl in the role of director was unusual in its time.

Moreover, the school had a policy of coeducation in all student offices. A boy and a girl must hold each office. This radical policy enforced coeducational sharing of power. It delivered a message that the school assumed boys and girls should have equal power, and that the school would be better if they did. As it happens, the Quaker Meeting for Worship, a one-hour silent meeting each week at which anyone might speak, had a correspondingly power-sharing feel to it. I found it a rather homespun event, since there was no pulpit and no male authority to preach to us as there had been at the other places of worship I had attended. I remember my particular embarrassment when women stood and spoke in Meeting. What did they know?

The pattern that I see here is that of a representative 1950s small-town, small-minded white middle-class "good girl" challenging everyone who was trying to give her a democratic and, in fact, a global education. Through internalized sexism and classism, I was rejecting teaching that offered us lateral answers to the question of who was competent, who was important, who had knowledge. The answer was everybody. Mr. Burton, the physics teacher, put it in so many words when he said, on the first day of class, "Physics is nothing but common sense wrapped around things you've seen all of your life. Ever since you were a baby hitting balls around your playpen, you have understood inertia and momentum. I just give you the names." So we were already in physics, and it was already in us. He made it seem as though we could all "do physics," because we already had. He also had us build batteries before we studied electricity, on the theory that in this way the boys would not feel they started out ahead of the girls, with a male affinity for science.

Mr. Burton seemed to me "too nice" for a Physics teacher. I heard that in another school a physics teacher said, "Physics is like Mt. Everest. Only a few of you will make it." I thought that made sense. Physics required heroism, and only a few survivors would live to tell the tale. In that other school students indeed fell off the mountain of physics, and if they lived to tell the tale, they compared their wounds, slings, casts, and scars, but they didn't love physics. Mr. Burton had a way of producing students who entered math and science fields, and my very shy lab partner, Ken Wilson, went on to win the Nobel Prize in Physics. It was not Mr. Burton's aim to produce Nobelists, but to be enabling for all of us. Everybody should be engaged and everybody should know that they brought to physics the authority of their own experience, even their infant experience, in the physical world. Now when I hear continual top-down comparisons made between industrialized nations and other nations, or between technological cultures and more indigenous cultures, I remember how the strong base of knowledge in all people was recognized by my Quaker teachers in a way that was impressive and exemplary for global education.

THE CHALLENGE FOR TEACHERS

This kind of education need not be confined to private schools. What it requires is the professional development of teachers who have cultivated a global sensibility or, in some cases, merely been given permission to bring their global sensibilities into school. Will this nation's domestic culture dare to produce students and teachers who practice thinking and connecting laterally? I think it is possible. It takes courage and imagination to bring to schooling more than we were taught to bring. But I feel that our current crises call for repair of a system that has settled for solipsism and a narrowly functional definition of citizenship that produces people who are employable and do not ask broader questions.

Moreover, I have found that teachers suffer from the same confinements that their students do. Many long to repair the damage done to them by the requirement that they leave their whole selves at home each day and teach from a very narrow segment of their perceptions and capacities, which too often means preparing students for standardized tests and unspeculative, normative ways of thinking. Though it may be hard to change schools and educational ideals, I have found through my experience that it is not so hard for teachers themselves to change if they feel they are recovering something they lost: their human breadth and their longing to help shape a world that is not torn apart.

For the last two decades, I have been working on professional development of teachers from my base at the Wellesley College Center for Research on Women. My main work is with the National SEED Project on Inclusive Curriculum, which I founded 17 years ago and have been codirecting with Emily Style since 1987. SEED stands for Seeking Educational Equity and Diversity. The program establishes teacher-led seminars in K–12 schools. Each seminar involves 10 to 20 committed teachers who meet each month to discuss questions like "What are we teaching?" and "What messages does our teaching deliver with regard to gender, race, class, culture, region, nation, and the world? What outcomes do we want of education? What works for students' and our own growth and development? Can we give our students a more complete picture than we were given ourselves, of the self and the world in their many dimensions? How can we make school climate, teaching methods, and curricula more gender-fair, multicultural, and global?" SEED seminars are powerful, and teachers are deeply changed by them. In some ways they resemble the format and assumptions of Quaker Meeting about the worth of all participants. They create space in which everybody speaks. There is no leading authority and there are no required texts, though there are piles of resources of many kinds. Teachers bring the authority of their own experience. They bring their life stories. The facilitators, whom we prepare for these seminars, receive many books and materials and videos, but it is up to them whether they want to use any of these. When teachers are in lateral spaces psychologically and are allowed to have their own conversations about what they know without outside pressure, then I think SEED replicates some elements of my Quaker schooling: comparative curriculum, reflective listening, and empowering assumptions about where knowledge resides.

But SEED seminars do not depend on any one spiritual tradition, and they improve on my own Quaker experience by teaching systemic seeing. They counter the usual U.S. ideology of individualism, in which the individual is seen as the unit of society, and the belief is that whatever one ends up with is what one wanted, worked for, earned, and deserved. (SEED seminars acknowledge systems of power working both within our psyches and in the world outside us. They call forth participants' own deep experience of power. In the balance between testifying to one's own experience and hearing the testimony of others, those qualities that I define as belonging to a capacity for global citizenship are brought forth. The technique that I have named Serial Testimony is particularly relevant to global perspectives. Each member of a group speaks in turn, within a set amount of time, very often 1 minute, or at most 3 minutes. During a serial testimony there is no interruption, no "cross-talk." After a serial testimony there is no debate. The aim is to speak and to listen, to hear and be heard, to compare, contrast, and deepen one's understanding of oneself and others. The modes of Serial Testimony undercut politics-as-usual. For educators, they provide a rare and welcome relief from faculty meetings and other forums in which the talkers talk, the listeners listen, and a general feeling of malaise prevails.

SEED seminars have now been led in the United States, Canada, Latin America, and 10 Asian countries, and may be led in any language with any materials. Many international schools that had an entirely U.S.–based curriculum before teachers engaged in SEED seminars have developed curricula, including language study, that are respectful of their host countries. On the more immediate level, within the seminar, the respectful interactive mode includes everyone of every nationality and cultural group as an authority on his or her own experience. Cultural chasms are bridged in SEED seminars. By balancing what codirector Emily Style calls "the scholarship on the shelves" with "the scholarship in the selves," they do inner and outer work. The program was devised by women and bears the imprint of our plural socialization. It reflects the balance of self and other that is asked of all people doing relational tasks. In another metaphor of Emily Style, the curriculum is like an architectural structure built around students. Ideally it provides a balance of "windows" out to the experience of others and "mirrors" of the students' own reality and validity. When curriculum serves as both "window" and "mirror," students are helped to become whole-souled, complex people. I imagine them as potential citizens of the world, having developed both identities of their own and interconnectedness with others. We have found that when the curriculum serves students as both "window" and "mirror," their alienation and anger decrease, together with their violence toward themselves and others.

INTERACTIVE PHASES AND GLOBAL CITIZENSHIP EDUCATION

United States educational institutions merely replicate the power relations of the rest of U.S. society unless we intervene with correctives. One corrective lens that SEED seminars often use is a Phase Theory I developed in 1983. It is a typology called "Interactive Phases of Curricular and Personal Re-Vision." I devised it after observing changes in college faculty members as they brought Women's Studies perspectives into their liberal arts courses.

I saw that traditionally trained white faculty members in any discipline were likely to move from what I called a Phase I frame of mind, which is womanless and all white, to a Phase II frame of mind, which admits "exceptional others" to the discipline, but only on the terms already laid down. Both frames of mind are challenged by what I identified as Phase III thinking, in which all women, and men of color, are seen as a problem, anomaly, absence, or victim, both in the academic world and in the aspect of the world that the discipline encompasses. Phase III is about coming to see systemically, and to understand local and global issues of, racism, sexism, classism, homophobia, anti-Semitism, nationalism, militarism, colonialism, and other kinds of power dynamics.

I see Phase III as an improvement on the womanless and all-white Phase I and the "exceptional others" flavor of Phase II. It is far wider and more accurate than teaching based on the ideology of individualism. It observes power systems and brings in issues of justice and care. It calls for and inspires action, including intellectual action. But Phase III can be polarizing and get arrested in victim studies. It can reduce people who suffer into mere cyphers with deficit identities. The systemic vision of Phase III makes an important advance into analysis of global problems, injustices, and maldistribution of goods and resources. But its stories can all sound the same, as in oppressor/oppressed; victims/victimizers; winner/losers.

Phase III improves when it partakes of, and rests on, the detailed narratives, the moving, grounded, daily, and plural stories of Phase IV, the phase of experience, everyone's experience, anywhere in the world. In Phase IV everyone is a knower. Everyone's daily life is history, politics, literature, drama, economics, psychology, and ecology. Within Phase IV, binary thinking is seen as too simple.

The four first interactive phases point toward an eventual Phase V: a version in which the world of knowledge is redefined and reconstructed to include us all, which I consider will take us 100 to 200 years to conceive, depending on the political choices the world makes in this and coming decades. I feel that we desperately need thinking that goes back and forth across the interface between Phase III issues and Phase IV experience, that is, in the interface between systemic issues of power and policy, seen abstractly, and the actual poignant stories of human beings' textured, relational, and interdependent lives as makers and menders of the fabric of life.

Most of education in the United States at present is stuck in Phases I and II. Standardized testing has intensified the value placed on womanless and all-white versions of reality, with a few "exceptions" allowed in. Phase I is about studying government, management, laws, wars, and winners, whether in the arts, sciences, or social sciences. Phase I courses ignore almost all of the world's population. In Phase II, the standardized textbooks bring in a few "others" who are seen as unlike their kind and therefore worth studying. The standardized tests bring in Frederick Douglass or Harriet Tubman, neither as living the actual daily life of an enslaved person, and each seen as modeling heroism in a way that more of their people "should have done." Though the United States in the last three decades paid lip service to critical thinking as a skill to be developed in students, and though it relates to what I see as the need for minds that can compare and contrast evidence from many sources, in recent years the call has been for basic literacy, with no attention paid at all to developing analytical minds, which of course might turn countercultural. Preparation for standardized testing squeezes out both the Phase III critical faculties and the Phase IV method in which student voices may be heard bringing in their own experience. These suppressions are no accident within an administration working toward centralized control. For if students or teachers are encouraged to tell what they know, their deep memories will lead them away from single and simple loyalties and right/wrong views of the world.

As I have written in my interactive Phase Theory, stories told by those who go back to their early childhood reveal that the multicultural globe is interior; the multicultural worlds are in us as well as around us. Early cultural conditioning trained each of us as children to shut off awareness of certain groups, voices, abilities, and inclinations, including the inclination to be with many kinds of children. Continents we might have known were closed off or subordinated within us. The domains of personality that remain can and do fill the conceptual space like colonizing powers. But a potential for pluralized understanding remains in us; the moves toward reflective consciousness come in part from almost-silenced continents within ourselves. Greater diversity of curriculum reflects not just the exterior multicultural world but the interior self that in early childhood was aware of, and attuned to, many varieties of experience. Recovery of that connectedness is a powerful aid to global citizenship. It can be a source of disorientation and anxiety, even shock, when one first remembers early connectedness that we were made to break off, as our educations or families shaped us for narrower class, race, and ethnic lives than our hearts inclined to.

Phase IV teaching dares to bring students' experience into the classroom and to derive new understanding from hitherto excluded or overlooked sources. Phase IV is the only frame of mind within the first four in my typology in which the student's own life counts. In its ability to educate and engage students, Phase IV goes far beyond the top-down oppressiveness of Phase I, the "exceptional others" framework of Phase II, and the focus on disembodied issues and polarities of Phase III.

Most traditionally trained white teachers started and continue to teach within the framework in which they were themselves taught: Phase I monoculturalism, in which U.S. white culture is the chief reality. In this frame of mind a teacher is oblivious of the racial and gender elements in his or her actual life, and ignores her/his Phase III issues and Phase IV relational experience while doing his or her paid work. Most teachers teach about conflict and wars, and accept bullying on the playground, or sexual harassment in the hallways, while they think of themselves as desiring peace. There is a gap between the avowed ideals of being peaceful and the actual practice of teaching, with teachers operating as if vertical conflict were inevitable and hierarchical competition were the only logical framework within which schooling could occur. Jane Roland Martin's call for the three C's of care, concern, and connection to balance the three R's of reading, writing, and 'rithmetic has scarcely been answered.

In SEED seminars, when we ask teachers to remember vivid vignettes from their own schooling as children and teenagers, nearly all of the memories are negative, and nearly all involve competition, loss, humiliation, and mortification. When the exercise shifts and we request that they recall positive moments from their own schooling, what they usually remember is working together, in connection, on projects, or sitting in peaceful places, talking. Their positive memories rarely involve beating others or winning, but they do sometimes involve pushing oneself beyond one's usual limits. If educators learn from such testimony and wish to work for a world that is peaceful, they will arrange to balance the win-lest-you-lose paradigm that schooling now takes for granted as "normal" with a paradigm emphasizing students' growth and development in connection. Most schoolchildren testify that they like to work on collaborative projects more than they like to work alone. Recently many schoolchildren have been greatly interested in Internet hookups with children of other countries. They are responding to global education.

HOPE FOR THE FUTURE

Writing this chapter during the spring of 2003 is very taxing because of the disconnect I feel between the ideal of educating U.S. students for global citizenship and the behavior of the U.S. government. To me, U.S. citizenship does not feel equated with God's particular approval. I see the United States as a place with a rare and wonderful dream of unity in diversity and a promise of the good life that has not yet been realized within its boundaries. I see the "American Dream" as set back severely by the acts of the Bush administration. It has enforced white, male-led Euro-American power and class dominance, when we need more global unity in diversity to hold the international fabric together. I feel that the Iraq war and its many costs do violence to the daily work of upkeep and maintenance everywhere, even in the United States. I fear that the United States's "good vs. evil," "us against them" thinking has weakened global cohesiveness over the long term, disrespecting men and women all over the world, rupturing the fabric of trust and the hope of more tolerant life between differing religions and cultures. It assumes the top-down, either/or Phase I model of life as War: every warrior for himself; every group of warriors for themselves; women and children can deal with their terrors and trials alone, while being expected to take care of daily provisioning for all of us behind the scenes. Though some women are in the U.S. armed services, these are wars conceived by and led by men. The U.S. media present women in the armed services as borrowed from their families; the media do not present generals as borrowed from their families.

While the situation in the United States in the first few years of the 21st century feels like living with an abusive, unbalanced, controlling father who is a bully at home and a bully in the neighborhood, I take hope from numerous sources. One is the interest of many U.S. citizens in wisdom from indigenous and non-Western cultures, including Asian cultures. Learning from people of color in the United States and learning from Asian people in Asia has given me a feeling of hopefulness, as they teach from a less exclusive base of thinking and acting. There is not such a sense of spiritual or social loneliness, nor such stratification based on money and possessions. Acquisition and greed are not such prime values, and the sense of community seems to me far stronger than in the communities of white capitalism that I know best, in which "community" was and still seems to me an empty, disembodied idea. In U.S. African-American, Latino, Native, and Asian-American cultures, I feel that the sense of community is stronger than in my white worlds. The United States has had increasing opportunities to study and learn from more plural value systems and skills, as the schools and the society have become more diverse in their populations. Usually the differences I see in cultures less powerful than my own correspond to values I was taught to hold as a woman in my particular part of patriarchal white U.S. culture. In doing multicultural study I am both revising what I see I am and recovering some of what I was encouraged to give up to fit into the place designated for me in U.S. social and gender structures.

Another source of hope for me is the change toward global education that has slowly but very surely occurred at Wellesley College, where I work. Though Wellesley is not very self-conscious or even verbal about its changes, they are remarkable to me. Nearly half of the students are U.S. students of color or international students who come from some 40 nations. Courses are offered in many languages. Eight or nine religious faiths from around the world are mentioned in the weekly calendar of events. Performance groups and social organizations have many cultural bases. Consultants, lecturers, and visitors come from around the world. New faculty members are hired from outside the United States. Curricula have become more and more international, cross-cultural, and serious about women. Women's Studies is thriving. The values of the college have shifted over the last 50 years, from promoting education for women who would marry powerful white men to promoting the development of students who will matter to themselves and to others in the world. I would not claim that the students are global citizens in the sense that I have defined global citizenship. The values of soloistic behavior, materialism, and personal power once conditioned chiefly into men are strong in the sensibilities of the female students I work with. But they are being educated to know that there is more out in the world than their individual ambitions will encompass or affect for the better. I think their frames of reference and values will widen in later years, as mine did, in part because those teachers of my 15-year-old self did not give up on me. I take as a given, now, that I should not give up on young people even if they do not want to become global citizens. Neither did I.

I was also very heartened by a poem and the woman who wrote it at the time of the inauguration of William Jefferson Clinton as President of the United States in 1992. It seemed wonderful to me that Clinton asked Maya

Angelou to write the inaugural poem, which she entitled *On the Pulse of the Morning*. The poem's global dimensions were spiritually uplifting to me. I remembered Robert Frost reciting his sonnet "The Gift Outright" at the time of John Kennedy's inauguration. Beautiful though it seemed to me, I found it on rereading to be deeply racist in its assumption that this land was empty until English people arrived. I saw Frost's poem as ignorant in a characteristic U.S. history textbook way. Its language was intricately filled with legalistic double meanings about deeds and ownership of the land. By contrast, Maya Angelou used as her primary metaphors The Rock, The River, and The Tree, which are in all lands and speak to all people. She invoked all of the peoples who live or lived in the United States and in every other culture in the world. She recognized deep suffering and inhumanity, and also looked to a new morning. That a poem of such reach and power would grace the inauguration of a U.S. president gave me and others whom I spoke with a great surge of hope in the future of the world.

Another source of hope for me has been the four U.N. Women's conferences of 1975, 1980, 1985, and 1995. The sharp divisions between the two sections of each signals to me that change is possible. In the official U.N. conference, women represent their nations' governments, or are represented by men in those governments, and the arguments and contentions are predictable and orchestrated by rules, rights, privileges, and responsibilities of membership in one's nation and in the conference. But in the Non-governmental Forum, women come together with much more of a sense of a shared and global agenda. In 1995 thirty thousand women came to the Forum in Beijing. I would trust them to run the world far more than I trust our present leaders, and to devise global education that would help us to live together better. Of course the women contend and fight, but the underlying plural sense of holding and being held in the midst of complexities is there. Our deep training is against either/or thinking and the violence it leads to. Since women and our dependents are the majority of any population and have had at least half of the world's lived experience, with responsibility for so many beyond ourselves, I feel we could in the aggregate be decent global judges of wise distribution of assets. Our policy concerns and skills have certainly been visible at these United Nations conferences. I used to scorn, as inefficient, the bureaucratic U.N. processes of inching toward a plural and multicultural agreement. Now I wonder how the world will survive without these U.N. processes and the empowerment of women's perspectives within them, which was started off so many years ago by the plural imagination and inclusive vision of Eleanor Roosevelt.

That we as a nation moved, for a while, into more global thinking than we had 50 years ago, before the U.N. was founded, is a source of hope for me despite the Bush administration's incapacity and disregard for plural understanding and its lack of intercultural skill. Its ignorance of other cultures reminds me of a more benign moment in the 1950s when my retired uncle from Middlebury, Connecticut, invited me to join him and his wife for a meal at the stately Savoy Hotel in London on the way home from their first trip outside the United States. In a booming voice heard all over the red-velvet Victorian dining room, my uncle proclaimed, "I've been all over Europe, seen seeenteen capitals in twenty one days, and I don't think they've improved on us in any way, shape, or form!" His wife sat silently. He seemed to me a stunningly ignorant, loud, rich, blind American. He was very badly educated. The White House today is not about lessening arrogance, ignorance, greed, chauvinism, or patriarchy through education. But educators themselves can still choose to change the mindset and heartset of the system that produced my uncle and his silent wife. They can, among other efforts, work to bring out her voice, so that a man does not speak for both parties. In her voice I think I would have heard at the very least that beyond her husband there were other people in those 17 capitals of Europe.

I remember my schoolteachers' fears of the House Committee on Un-American Activities in the 1950s. Citizens accused of having communist leanings were blacklisted and lost jobs and public protection. Many teachers who refused to take loyalty oaths to the United States were fired. At the time I did not know why my teachers were quite so upset. In response to many policies of the Bush administration, the forces for repression of dissent are strong, and once again many college students seem to be ignorant of why any of their professors are upset about silencing of academic discussion of our foreign policy, and about the silencing of commentary on the Iraq war's local and international race, gender, and class dimensions. Most students have trouble seeing the war or U.S. government policy globally or systemically. In this regard they are good students of what the culture at large has taught them: that there are no large power systems in or around us. I feel that to educate global citizens we will need to support teachers to prepare students and themselves not only for what the United States has considered "standard," but also for "nonstandard" awareness and appreciation of the connected global ecosystems we are in, and the many ways in which human beings can make meaning of our lives without killing each other.

Global travel can be a great introduction or reinforcement to global awareness, though it has class parameters and limitations. Closer to home, even travel down the road can pluralize the mind and heart. In this technological age, much vicarious experience can be had through Internet travel and international exchanges. But students need to develop critical faculties with which to see, and heartfelt connections with which to feel what they are traveling into. In school, sometimes it is the heartfelt trust of a teacher in the worth of a student in a completely local situation that produces a faith within the student that he or she is connected to the world in a way that matters, and that the world is worth caring about. Often it is the day-by-day exchanges that open our capacities to care about, seek to understand, and work for that which is beyond our immediate view, that which is larger than us, but includes and holds us. The global sense for belonging and making spaces for all to belong can be developed close to home by teachers bringing the wholeness of their emotions and capacities into classrooms, unafraid to help students also to develop the plural capacities and the wide-ranging awareness that caretakers absolutely depend on when they work for the decent survival of all.

CHAPTER 2

The Integration of Conflict Resolution into the High School Curriculum: The Example of Workable Peace

Stacie Nicole Smith & David Fairman

"I've learned that conflict is not what causes the problems in the world; it's the way that people deal with these conflicts that causes the problems."

—Ninth-Grade Workable Peace Student

THREE WEEKS AFTER SEPTEMBER 11, 2001, students in Ms. Gearhy's 10th-grade World History I class in Newton, Massachusetts, put aside their planned lessons on ancient China to hold a dialogue about appropriate U.S. responses to terrorism. The U.S. response was an issue that touched them all, and emotions ran high. To guide the class in effective listening and communication skills, they used a framework for understanding and dealing with conflict created by *Workable Peace*, a curriculum project of the Consensus Building Institute.

The students were given four perspectives on possible U.S. responses to September 11—each represented by two recently published opinion pieces from newspapers or journals—and asked to choose the perspective that most resembled their own. They were then asked, in four groups based on perspective, to map out their underlying perspectives on the conflict in order to better understand what was most important to them in this dialogue by focusing on their interests, beliefs, emotions, and identities. Finally, the students all came together to express their needs, concerns, and beliefs, and to compare and contrast their own perspectives with those of their classmates.

In the discussion, students not only defended their own deeply felt views but were also asked to listen to, restate, and acknowledge the needs and concerns underlying their classmates' perspectives. Rather than scoring points or reaching agreements, the goal of this discussion was to develop a better understanding of how and why Americans might legitimately disagree on what the United States should do in response to September 11. Among the skills that the students practiced were explaining their views clearly, listening actively, acknowledging others' legitimate concerns, brainstorming options that reflected the needs of all points of view, and examining how the key issues might be resolved in ways that would meet the primary needs and concerns of others. Thus the students were introduced to a model of conflict resolution that they could use to process not only the crisis of September 11, but one that they could draw on when examining conflicts throughout the school year.

Effective Conflict Resolution Education (CRE) should begin in elementary school and continue through secondary school, focusing at each grade level on developmentally appropriate skills and behaviors. Elementary and middle schools provide settings for learning many foundational CRE concepts and behaviors. High school is particularly appropriate for the higher-level integration of knowledge and skills that students need to understand intergroup conflict in history and society, and to draw lessons that apply to their lives and current events. Cognitively, teenagers can explore and analyze complex social issues. Developmentally, they are seeking and being cast into adult social roles and learning how their membership in ethnic, economic, and cultural groups will shape those roles. Academically and socially, adolescents are studying and experiencing conflict and find themselves confronting decisions about their own responses (Crawford and Bodine 1996). High schools, therefore, can appropriately and effectively teach young people to understand, synthesize, and apply the behaviors and skills associated with tolerance, conflict management, and effective citizenship.

Despite this enormous educational opportunity, many high schools lack the mandate and the tools to teach such skills. This is true even in academic disciplines where issues of intergroup conflict are most directly addressed: history and social studies. According to the National Council for the Social Studies, "learning the content and thinking skills necessary for students to make public policy decisions, operate successfully in a society to build consensus, and learn to negotiate and manage differences have been the bulkheads of the field" (Soley 1996). Yet numerous studies of social studies curricula and lessons show minimal effort to promote dialogue or negotiation skills on controversial topics (Goodlad 1984, McNeil 1986). Most high school social studies classes do not teach students to analyze multiple sources of conflict or to see conflict from multiple perspectives. Most core classroom texts do not assess critically the strategies that leaders and groups have used to deal with conflict, or ask students to examine alternative responses and evaluate their potential costs and benefits. And rarely do students put themselves into the shoes of primary actors in historical conflicts, to try out for themselves different ways to meet their needs and uphold their values.

One high school global studies text offers this description of the colonization of the Americas:

> The capture of Montezuma resulted in the Aztec ruler giving Cortes huge quantities of gold objects in hope of gaining his freedom. Montezuma was eventually killed, and his golden treasure was melted down into bullion bars. Within three years, warfare and disease destroyed the Aztec trading and tributary empire. Cortes, in the name of the Spanish monarchy, became the new ruler of Mexico. (Willner et al. 1995, 188)

Traditionally, the conflicts presented in history and current events—between peoples, states, and social groups—are presented as facts and events, with little effort to examine the complex underlying dynamics. Without an opportunity for structured and critical learning about intergroup conflict, students often draw their understanding from history's victors. The lessons they often learn include: group identities are fixed, conflict is usually zero-sum, and violence and coercion are not only common but often effective ways—maybe the only ways—to deal with intergroup conflict.

THE IMPORTANCE OF INTEGRATING CONFLICT RESOLUTION SKILLS INTO ACADEMIC CONTENT

For 30 years, concerned educators have been developing ways to teach conflict management skills to students in public schools. One common approach is teaching conflict resolution as an extracurricular activity (e.g., a peer mediation program) or as an elective course (e.g., negotiation skills training), using content and examples from interactions with teachers, friends, and family. Such strategies can be called "stand-alone" or "process curriculum" because they are not designed to teach specific academic content in conjunction with conflict management skills.

Stand-alone programs have been found to offer significant benefits, especially in the elementary and middle school grades. However, this approach has several limitations. First, any program that is separate and distinct from the core academic focus of schools is vulnerable to short-term shifts in faculty and student interest. The vulnerability of such programs only grows as the spread of high-stakes standardized testing increases pressures to cover content. This is especially true in urban and lower-income schools, where testing pressures are often coupled with budget constraints on electives and other curricular extras, and courses and activities focused on teaching social and civic skills are squeezed out (Neill and Gayler 2001).

Second, even when such stand-alone programs remain, they run the risk of appearing "extra" to the students. If such courses or units are not given equal value in relation to academics by the school culture, students are also less likely to take them seriously. Students learn that what matters is the material on the tests required for graduation. Thus, mediation and conflict resolution programs, when devoid of academic content and disconnected from the knowledge of their core courses, become lower priority in the minds of students.

Connected to this is a third, and possibly most important, limitation of nonintegrated approaches to civic and social skills. If we want to affect the way young people think about and deal with conflict, we need to do so within the context of the conflicts they learn about in school. Lessons about conflict are taught within the academic curriculum but are often lessons normalizing violence and coercion. Conflict management skills taught in isolation are unlikely to overcome the assumptions and beliefs about conflict embedded in traditional social studies and history curricula. For all of these reasons, conflict resolution education is most effective when it is integrated into the academic curriculum.

STRATEGIES FOR INTEGRATING CONFLICT RESOLUTION SKILLS WITH THE CORE CURRICULUM

If stand-alone approaches to teaching conflict resolution are risky, is there an alternative that schools, teachers, and students are more likely to embrace and sustain? While there are not many social studies and history curricula that explicitly address intergroup conflict on a general, sociological level, there are a few curriculum enrichment programs that have succeeded in integrating new ways to teach about intergroup conflict and conflict resolution in a significant number of schools.

One of the best-developed of these is the high school curriculum Facing History and Ourselves (at http://www.facing.org). This multifaceted social studies curriculum uses the Holocaust as an extended case study to illustrate a general pattern of intergroup conflict escalation from the historical origins of stereotyping, prejudice, and racism, through socially discriminatory behavior and localized violence, to legalized exclusion, state-sanctioned violence, and ultimately genocide. Other school curricula focus more specifically on issues of prejudice and bias. Still other curricula focus broadly on "peace education," teaching philosophies of peace and nonviolence through readings in religion and philosophy and case studies on the nonviolent resolution of particular conflicts.

There is evidence suggesting that these integrative approaches succeed in teaching conflict resolution concepts and skills while also helping students learn facts and concepts in history and social studies. One study of an integrated multiyear program found significantly higher achievement and retention for students who had received the integrated program, versus those students who had received only the academic content (Johnson and Johnson 1994). Other studies have yielded similar findings (Aber, Brown, and Henrich 1999). Reviewing five recent studies on integrating conflict resolution and academic coursework, Stevahn noted that students who received integrated lessons

> . . . expressed more positive attitudes toward conflict; scored significantly higher on academic achievement and retention tests aimed at assessing critical thinking and reasoning; [and] transferred the ability to use the conflict resolution procedures learned in one academic discipline to analyze the meaning of material in a different academic discipline, which resulted in higher achievement across disciplines. (Stevahn 1998)

There are, of course, limits to what any one curriculum integration program can achieve in regard to the depth of student learning. The integration of one project into one class is unlikely to effect profound changes in student behaviors. And even a fully integrated conflict resolution curriculum that students learn across several classes over several years may not be enough to make our schools or communities more peaceful or democratic (Brion-Meisels 1995). Nevertheless, the classroom is the central feature of the school experience, and creating "peaceable classrooms" is clearly a critical step toward building peaceable schools (Lantieri and Patti 1996).

OVERVIEW OF WORKABLE PEACE

The *Workable Peace* curriculum aims to teach general concepts and skills of conflict analysis and management in the context of historical and current events selected for relevance to high school social studies and history curricula. In this section, we explore the *Workable Peace* curriculum as a model for discussing what students learn about conflict, how they learn it, and the difference this can make.

Workable Peace is based at the Consensus Building Institute (CBI) in Cambridge, Massachusetts, a nonprofit organization dedicated to improving the theory and practice of public dispute resolution. The project was created and piloted in 1997 by an advisory board and staff of dispute resolution professionals—psychologists, political scientists, urban planners, philosophers—working with high school educators. Their goal was to translate state-of-the-art knowledge about the nature of conflict and conflict management into clear, practical, and evocative materials and pedagogy for high school social studies and history teachers and students. The *Workable Peace* curriculum has three main components: a conceptual framework, historical role-plays, and civic learning projects that relate directly to students' lives.

The Framework

At the heart of the curriculum is the *Workable Peace Framework*, a one-page summary of conflict management concepts and skills that the curriculum aims to teach. The *Workable Peace Framework* (see Figure 2.1) is an attempt to synthesize and distill 40 years of knowledge from research and practice in intergroup conflict management. It incorporates academic and practitioner insights from fields of political science, social psychology, and multiparty negotiation into a one-page presentation of skills and behaviors.[1] It is designed to make conflict analysis accessible to teenagers and to provide a theoretical foundation for the more active, content-centered pieces of the curriculum.

Role-Play

The core tool for teaching the framework is a series of role-play units set in historical and current hot spots of intergroup conflict. Each unit centers on

FIGURE 2.1. Workable Peace Framework

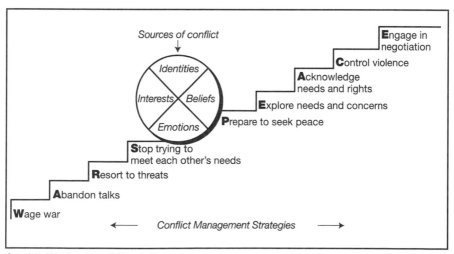

a major historical conflict that has been aligned with state and national curriculum standards for social studies, and challenges students to resolve the issues at stake in the conflict. The role-plays address conflict in ancient Greece, American 19th-century labor history, and the mid-20th-century civil rights movement, as well as the contemporary Middle East, Guatemala, Northern Ireland, and Rwanda.

Role-play is a type of learning by doing that allows participants an opportunity to develop direct experience with the content and skills being taught by taking on the personality and background of an individual or group and interacting with others in the context of a specific situation. Role-play provides an opportunity for learners to internalize concepts, principles, and ideas through lived experience and reflection, leading to changes in behaviors and actions (Dewey 1938). There are several educational theories about how this occurs, but all of them involve "a process of confronting our existing ideas about how and why certain things happen, breaking them down, and offering a new model or set of postulates to replace the old ones" (Susskind and Corburn 2000, 291).

It is one thing to know how to manage conflict, but quite another to act on this knowledge, particularly in difficult situations where your own needs are at stake, your core beliefs challenged, and your emotions intense. Practicing conflict management behaviors within a realistic role helps students to confront the psychological and interpersonal responses that are most difficult to manage in situations of real conflict. At the same time, role-play provides a safe setting that allows students to experiment, reflect, and give and receive feedback.

At the end of role-plays, teachers lead students through a debriefing. Students reflect on how well they met their own group's interests and upheld their values and identities, how well they did at reaching an agreement meeting the interests of all parties, how well they worked as a negotiating group, and what they would do differently next time. A skillful teacher can generate an enormous amount of learning about conflict and conflict resolution through the debriefing, drawing on examples of specific moments in the negotiation process.

Civic Learning

The curriculum's third part, civic learning projects, encourages teachers to connect themes and lessons from history to conflicts occurring in the world today and in students' lives. This approach is consistent with research on effective civic education, which shows that making explicit connections between historical and current situations is more likely to affect student behavior (Carnegie Corporation 2003, 23).

WHAT DO STUDENTS LEARN? HOW DO THEY LEARN IT? WHAT DIFFERENCE DOES IT MAKE?

Workable Peace is designed to provide students with opportunities to learn a broad set of social and civic skills for dealing with conflict, while learning social and historical facts and themes. This section highlights the social and civic skills that the curriculum integrates with historical and social studies content.

Conflict Analysis

When we are in a situation of conflict, we rarely stop to think about the multiple needs, concerns, and feelings that underlie the particular problem at hand. *Workable Peace* teaches students to understand the multiple causes of a conflict by taking conflicts apart and analyzing them piece by piece. The *Workable Peace Framework* names four core sources of conflict: interests (what we and they want), beliefs (our views and theirs about what should be, especially rights and values, and what is, especially perceptions of our histories and current situations), identities (who we and they are, especially as members of social groups), and emotions (what we and they feel). Students are taught to name and disentangle these key components of conflict, and use them to better understand the perceptions of opposing groups involved in conflict.[2]

Consider this example: In a lesson about the 1962 Cuban Missile Crisis, students were divided into two groups, and provided with letters and speeches from either Soviet Premier Nikita Khrushchev or U.S. President John F. Kennedy. The students used the documents to map out the sources of conflict—the interests, beliefs, emotions, and identities—from their perspective, in one column, and from their ideas of the other perspective in a second column (see Table 2.1). The two groups of students then reconvene to share their work, and the teacher puts the two finished charts side-by-side to form a four-column map of the conflict.

The ability to understand multiple sources underlying a conflict can benefit students in many ways. First, knowing what is driving you in a conflict helps you understand the reasons underlying what you want. This is called "moving from positions to interests." Khrushchev's position was to keep the missiles in Cuba, with one underlying interest of preventing a U.S. attack on Cuba. Second, clarifying interests and focusing on them creates many more possibilities for resolving conflicts (Fisher and Ury 1983). Khrushchev was ultimately able to meet his interest in preventing a U.S. attack on Cuba by gaining a noninvasion pledge from Kennedy in exchange for withdrawing the missiles.

TABLE 2.1. Cuban Missile Crisis: Comparative Map of the Core Sources of Conflict for Presidents Khrushchev and Kennedy

| | PERSPECTIVE OF KHRUSHCHEV | | PERSPECTIVE OF KENNEDY | |
	Us	THEM	Us	THEM
INTERESTS "We want because . . ."	• to defend Cuba's sovereignty • to help Cuba defend herself from U.S. attack • to support our international allies	• intimidation of USSR • to attack Cuba • no Russian influence in Cuba • removal of missiles	• to protect the U.S. from attack by USSR from Cuba • weapons removed from Cuba • no wish for war	• world domination • control of Cuba • ability to attack the U.S.
BELIEFS "We believe . . ."	• USSR's relationship with Cuba is not of U.S. concern • U.S. actions violate international law; ours do not • missiles in Cuba are defensive	• the U.S. can issue ultimatums and threats with impunity	• U.S. peace is endangered by these missiles • USSR is violating promises • U.S. protects the democratic and capitalist countries of the world	• USSR can deceive the U.S. • provocation will go unchallenged
EMOTIONS "We feel . . ."	• indignant • pushed • justified	• powerful • superior	• confident • strong • justified	• righteous
IDENTITIES "We are . . ."	• reasonable • supporters of Cuban freedom	• aggressors • imperialists • immoral	• peaceful • honest • patient • powerful • reasonable	• deceptive • aggressors

You may also find that you have interests, such as avoiding war, that conflict with other interests, beliefs, or identities. This analysis helps students to see the trade-offs that are made in any decision and encourages them to weigh and prioritize their needs. For President Kennedy, the deal with Khrushchev addressed the overriding U.S. interest in reducing the threat of a missile strike by the USSR. At the same time, the deal required trading off the U.S. interest in overthrowing Castro.

Conflict analysis may also highlight the role your emotions play in driving or escalating conflict, in ways that may work against your interests or values. During the Cuban Missile Crisis, both U.S. and Soviet decisionmakers felt intense fear and anger that several times threatened to derail the negotiation process and escalate the conflict. As students identify and discuss emotions that the decisionmakers felt, they begin to appreciate not only the importance of emotions in historical conflicts, but also how they handle their own emotions in conflicts.

By practicing conflict analysis, students develop a skill they can use on their own to deal with conflicts experienced around them and in their own lives. For example, one student wrote, "Now when I look at a conflict . . . I look at it with 'What are my interests? What are my values? What are my identities? What are their interests, their values, and their identities?' Do you use what we've learned on other things? Personally, I do. It's an easier way to break it down."

Perspective-Taking

Members of groups in conflict—especially long-standing and violent conflict—have a tendency to delegitimize, stereotype, and ultimately dehumanize their opponents. Negotiation based on partial and biased perception of other groups' interests and needs, in an atmosphere of deep animosity, is unlikely to be productive. Conversely, dialogue focused on understanding the other can begin to break down stereotypes; highlight shared interests, values, and identities; and lay the basis for productive negotiation (Fisher 2000; Kelman 1997; Rubin et al. 1994, 161–162).

Students using the *Workable Peace* curriculum begin developing perspective-taking skills during the conflict mapping activity described above by examining differences in how each group perceives itself and is perceived by others. Students can then consider the ways in which perceptions and misperceptions can make it more difficult to deal productively with conflict. This exercise allows them to develop an appreciation of the value of dialogue in clarifying each other's perspectives.

This point is made most clear during the role-plays when participants must confront the differing perspectives of their negotiating partners. Students have an opportunity to attempt taking the perspective of a negotiating partner and to see how doing so can help them meet their own interests. In the role-plays, students learn that it is impossible to develop solutions if they can't agree on what the conflict is about, or if they don't know what needs the other side is trying to achieve. Therefore, participants are encouraged to engage in a process of exploration, with the goal of understanding how each group sees the situation and what each group hopes to achieve in a resolution.

The value of perspective-taking has been made clear to us over and over again. In a study of our work with Israeli and Palestinian schools, Haifa University researchers found that after participating in *Workable Peace* role-plays on other historical conflicts, students demonstrated substantial changes in their ability to see the Israeli-Palestinian conflict through the eyes of the other. One example is performance on an assignment asking students to write about the Israeli-Palestinian conflict from the point of view of the other side. In the pretest and control groups, students could write little or nothing from the viewpoint of the other. At posttest, virtually all of the *Workable Peace* students were able to write with understanding and empathy from the other group's perspective (Lustig 2001).

Students in the United States have had similar responses about the value of this skill. One student reflected, "I feel I learned a significant amount about the importance of thinking about a situation through the perspective of another person. We must take time to think about what the people around us might be feeling about different situations. It is important not to assume that we know how they feel, but to try to explore their point of view in order to try to solve problems."

Listening and Communication Skills

Understanding is necessary but not sufficient for conflict resolution. *Workable Peace* also teaches the importance of acknowledging needs and rights (e.g., the right to exist or to self-determination; the need for a living wage or a minimum level of profitability). Acknowledgment has two functions: psychologically, mutual acknowledgment can have a powerful transformative effect by overturning deeply held assumptions about the intentions and beliefs of opposing groups; strategically, acknowledgment of specific needs and rights creates a framework for negotiation by setting out issues to be addressed (Kelman 1997).

During the role-play negotiations, there is often a turning point when a student voices the legitimacy of the needs, emotions, or experiences of a negotiating partner. Acknowledgment can dramatically increase willingness to work cooperatively or make trade-offs to resolve conflict. One student commented:

It was interesting in the Northern Ireland role play how the residents acknowledged the pains of the Orange Order and how they were getting hurt in the
struggle. This changed the attitude of the Orange Order. With this new attitude
the Orange Order seemed to try and give things up for the Catholics more readily.

With the help of a skilled teacher, the role-plays also teach other critical communication skills that have been identified for effective social and
civic interaction: active listening and asking questions, modifying tone of voice
and body language, dealing effectively with emotions, and reframing negative statements into positive statements (Raider 1995).

Negotiation Skills

Although poor communication dramatically increases the probability that
conflicts will continue or escalate, good communication, on its own, does
not necessarily lead to resolution (Krauss and Morsella 2000). Negotiation
skills such as assessing interests and alternatives, inventing options, making
trade-offs, and seeking objective criteria for decision-making can help parties translate understanding into concrete options and strategies for resolving issues that divide them. *Workable Peace* teaches a mutual-gains approach
to negotiation developed at the Harvard-MIT-Tufts Program on Negotiation (see especially CBI 2000; Fisher and Ury 1983; Sebenius 1992; Susskind
et al. 1999). Students learn and practice this approach during the role-plays,
where they attempt to find resolutions that offer their group more than the
alternative of continued conflict. In addition to effective preparation and
focusing on interests, key negotiation skills include inventing options and
making wise trade-offs to reach agreement.

As noted above, students need to move beyond mutual understanding to generate options that could be better for all parties than their alternatives outside of negotiation. *Workable Peace* teaches students to use a
"what if" approach. Rather than simply trading offers or criticizing each
other's proposals, students should be asking each other *why* they want
what they want and framing their proposals conditionally: "What if we
tried a different option that could work for me and—if I'm understanding
your interests—could work for you?" This approach makes the process of
inventing options collaborative rather than adversarial. Imagining multiple
alternatives fosters creativity because students are not yet seeking agreement, but rather brainstorming to look for possibilities worthy of further
development.

To illustrate, consider this example of students negotiating security arrangements in Hebron during the Middle East role-play. The group was
discussing two issues, control over the land in Hebron and maintaining

security for Israeli settlers living in the core areas of the city. Israeli and Palestinian governmental representatives, Israeli military, and Palestinian police all agreed that after a period of 5 years without violence, all control over land in Hebron would be given to the Palestinians. In addition, the Israeli military would withdraw completely from Hebron, leaving the settlers under Palestinian protection. The Israeli settlers were highly opposed to this agreement:

> *Settler:* If you get control of H2 area, why can't we keep the Israeli military to protect the settlers?
>
> *Palestinian Police:* We can't guarantee protection of Israelis within Hebron unless the military leaves. It's our city, and we aren't going to let you have Israeli control.
>
> *Settler:* But we don't trust you. You have to understand, the Palestinian Police is made up of former terrorists.
>
> *Palestinian Government:* Well, you're just going to have to trust us.
>
> *Israeli Military:* What if, during the five year transitional period, you were able to develop trust in the Palestinian police, while the Israeli Military remained in H2 and patrolled jointly with the Palestinian police?

In this example, the student playing the Israeli military role seeks to break a potential impasse and deal with mutual, deep-seated distrust by proposing a transitional period as a "what-if."

Negotiators may be very effective at creating options, yet still face great difficulty reaching a final agreement; they need to find some objective principles, standards, or criteria—meaning acceptable to all negotiators—to help them choose among the options. By integrating these negotiation skills through historically accurate role-plays, *Workable Peace* not only helps students gain a deeper understanding of a particular conflict, but also helps foster a range of civic and social aptitudes, including creative thinking, problem-solving, and moral reasoning. The benefits for students of integrating conflict resolution skills into their study of history include making decisions with others, discussing differences, solving problems, and dealing with emotions—in short, skills needed to participate effectively as democratic citizens. As one student wrote:

> The role play does aid in strengthening conflict-resolving characteristics in a person. We learn how to look at the conflict through the other person's eyes, what things are and aren't beneficial to say or do in the process, and we learn how to settle the conflict so that both sides are happy.

Civic Engagement and Skills

One of the *Workable Peace* curriculum's goals is to help students apply the concepts and skills learned through the *Workable Peace Framework* and role-plays to intergroup issues and conflicts in their schools and communities. The curriculum provides a number of tools and activities for civic learning. For example, our Northern Ireland role-play on the annual marching season, which often heightens tensions or leads to violence between Catholics and Protestants, has a civic learning activity that asks students to examine the debate over flying the Confederate flag in some Southern states. Our Boston school integration role-play concludes with an activity that asks students to consider arguments on the effects of integration on student learning in light of the current context of school integration in Boston in the early 21st century.

We also provide more general guidelines for teachers on how to make links from a historical activity to current events, school culture, and community issues. Those guidelines ask students to identify key stakeholders and issues in a particular conflict and to map the conflict sources and the strategies stakeholders are using. Students can do research on these issues in the library, on the Internet, or through interviews and opinion polls, as well as through attending public hearings and meetings in their communities. The *Workable Peace* Web site also has a current conflicts page, including information from multiple perspectives and study exercises that reinforces core concepts from the *Workable Peace Framework*.

CHALLENGES OF AND STRATEGIES FOR INTEGRATING CONFLICT MANAGEMENT

In our work with teachers and students on the *Workable Peace* project, we have experienced many successes. However, we have also come to recognize a number of constraints, barriers, and obstacles to integrating conflict resolution and civic skills into academic content. One major set of challenges to the successful implementation of any curricular program involves teachers' preparation to teach the concepts and skills. As both experience and numerous studies show, teachers' understanding of the material, pedagogical skill, motivation, and creativity have huge impacts on student learning. This is even more true with experiential learning materials like *Workable Peace* where the skills and the pedagogy may be quite different from what the teacher is accustomed to employing. Conflict resolution educator Ellen Raider observes, "Most adults in schools have had little preparation, training, or encouragement to manage their own conflicts cooperatively, let alone teach these skills to others" (Raider 1995). How can we expect teachers to teach conflict management skills when they have not been taught such skills themselves?

To get the most out of the curriculum, teachers must know not only how to logistically structure and manage the activities, but also how to watch for the teachable moments that arise during role-plays and guide student discussions about what they can learn from their experiences. To do this successfully, teachers not only need to understand the skills, they need opportunities to practice them. For this reason, we have emphasized the importance of comprehensive teacher training as preparation for implementing the *Workable Peace* curriculum. Our standard three-day institute has the dual purpose of introducing teachers to the skills of conflict management and preparing them to integrate the curriculum into their classrooms. At the workshops, teachers are challenged to integrate these new concepts and skills into their own understandings and behaviors as they simultaneously work to absorb the knowledge and pedagogy.

A more efficient and effective strategy for providing large numbers of teachers with the skills to institutionalize the teaching of conflict management would be to incorporate such preparation into preservice teacher education programs. Ideally, this would be integrated by using curriculum materials like *Workable Peace* in social studies methods courses. Teachers might also be offered role-plays set around typical conflicts they will experience in classrooms and meeting rooms.

Another serious challenge is the pressure to cover historical content. Most social studies and history teachers feel very constrained in the time they can spend on any one topic or theme. The pressure to skim the surface is a challenge to all approaches that use in-depth learning to teach analytic skills and interpersonal skills as well as facts.

One potential strategy is to use *Workable Peace* to cover a topic in depth, then leverage that experience to help students learn about other topics that cannot be covered in equal depth. For example, one U.S. history teacher introduces the *Workable Peace Framework* at the beginning of the year, and has students use it to analyze the sources of the American Revolution and how the strategies of the colonists and the British led to war. She then uses the framework when teaching about the Civil War; the Pullman strike role-play when teaching about labor conflict in the Gilded Age; and the framework again when covering the first and second world wars, the Cold War, and the civil rights movement.

Our experience with teachers of *Workable Peace* suggests that creative integration of conflict resolution skills can have very positive effects on student learning. In an independent evaluation of *Workable Peace*, teachers reported that student learning was deeper, lasted longer, and went far beyond the content for a particular historical event. Motivation to learn about other conflicts increased and students were likely to pay more attention to conflicts in current events (Donahue-Keegan and LaRusso 1999).

CONCLUSION

Perhaps the greatest challenge to teaching conflict management skills to teenagers is the "believability" factor. If students don't see the strategies they are studying reflected in their schools, communities, and world, it is much harder for them to imagine using these skills and tools themselves. Teaching peaceful strategies for solving world problems in times of war often feels like paddling upstream in a heavy current, and students often resist the lessons provided by their own simulated experiences, expressing cynicism and pointing to the more obvious unilateral, hierarchical, and power-based strategies they see around them. One example of this occurred in a school where many of the social studies teachers used *Workable Peace* activities in their courses while, simultaneously, the school was undergoing a very contentious and controversial restructuring process in which students felt their voices were not being heard. As a result, when students were asked about conflict management after doing a *Workable Peace* role-play, many students told us that they felt frustrated about their lack of voice in decisions that affect them. While they exhibited greater understanding of the dynamics of conflict, they seemed skeptical about the use of mutual-gains negotiation, since they didn't see this approach being used around them. The best strategy for addressing this challenge is to increase the practice of effective conflict management, consensus-building, and democratic decisionmaking in our classrooms, our schools, our communities, and our nation. We need to keep teaching conflict-management skills to students, but we also need to teach these skills to the adults in their lives. We can use civic learning projects to facilitate more civic engagement by high school students in their communities and their nations. We can increase opportunities for collaborative problem-solving within classrooms and schools, and promote more effective use of schools as forums for exploring and addressing conflicts in the communities they serve. We need to work at many levels to promote workable, peaceful solutions to the many conflicts that we face in a world where global citizens will be called upon to solve global problems. Integrating conflict resolution skills into the curriculum is one key strategy for advancing that goal.

NOTES

1. The primary academic and applied sources for the development of the *Workable Peace Framework* and supporting exercises include CBI 2000, Fisher 1993,

Fisher and Ury 1983, Horowitz 1985, Jervis 1978, Kelman 1997, Lake and Rothchild 1998, Lax and Sebenius 1993, Rubin et al. 1994, Schelling 1960, and Tellis et al. 1997.

2. The four sources named in the *Workable Peace Framework* are a synthesis of the literature on conflict factors, drawing especially from Fisher 2000, 168–173; Horowitz 1985, Chs. 4–5; Kelman 1997, 194–208; Rubin et al. 1994, Ch. 2; Tellis et al. 1997, 77–86.

CHAPTER 3

Place-Based Education to Preserve the Earth and Its People

Nel Noddings

IN WESTERN SOCIETIES TODAY, education is usually aimed at producing young citizens who can function effectively anywhere in the postindustrial world. This emphasis may be a mistake. Not only does such an education deprive young people of the knowledge they need to care for and appreciate the places in which they grow up; it also fails to provide them with an understanding of what place means in the lives of people in other parts of the globe.

In this brief discussion of place-based education, I look at four major aspects of the human connection to place: 1) the political/psychological—how a psychological attachment to place affects political attitudes; 2) the environmental—how care for one's natural surroundings may contribute to a commitment to care for the whole Earth; 3) the relation between local and global citizenship—how educational strategies can use love of place to develop knowledge and skills useful in the larger world; and 4) love of place and human flourishing—what place can mean in individual lives.

POLITICAL/PSYCHOLOGICAL CONSIDERATIONS

It is not my intention here to discuss territorial battles and the constant shifting of political boundaries that result from national and tribal warfare. World history and political geography are filled with such accounts. What I want to do is to consider how attachment to place affects political attitudes and how an understanding of this connection might guide more sensitive political decisions.

Consider, as a prime example, the current Israeli-Palestinian conflict. Probing the situation for deep underlying factors and concentrating on just one—attachment to place—does not imply an attempt to justify the enormous harm that these groups have inflicted on each other. Rather, the purpose is to understand one significant aspect of the problem and to suggest that careful attention to it should guide attempts at resolution.

Katherine Platt describes the stages of political conflict arising from the loss of place. The first generation, exiled from its homeplace, grieves for the lost home in every detail. Remembrance and longing characterize its attitude, its very life. Everything about the homeplace seems vivid, and the longing is for that specific place exactly as it lingers in memory.

Generations after the first have a very different experience. Platt writes:

> The literal places of origin so copiously mourned by the older generation became generalized and symbolic. Peasant class position and consciousness was replaced by working class position and consciousness. Clan and village solidarity gradually crumbled and has slowly been replaced by a Palestinian national identity. (Platt 1996, 125)

With this sense of national identity and the continued separation from a symbolic homeplace came outrage, demands made in the name of rights, and an angry attempt to justify horrendous acts in the name of national justice.

Symbolic attachment to place also drives many Israelis. For them, the separation is many centuries longer and, thus, almost wholly symbolic. Indeed, attachment to *this* place—so newly realized—is often compensation for the violent eviction from another loved place. Not everyone is wise enough to understand the power of symbolic attachment. Elie Wiesel demonstrates this wisdom. Asked by a reporter where he felt most at home, he responded: "In Jerusalem—when I am not in Jerusalem" (Wiesel 1996, 28).

One can imagine an education that would help both Palestinian and Israeli children understand their mutual longing for a homeplace. Can a homeplace be shared, or must ideological substitutes for that longing demand dominion of one group over the other?

We cannot solve a conflict of such depth and complexity in a few short paragraphs, but we can do what Martin Buber described as the teacher's task: "That raising of the finger, that questioning glance, are his genuine doing" (Buber 1965, 90). Thus we might raise a warning finger to question the wisdom of destroying homes or exiling the relatives of criminals. There is no possible justification for the deliberate killing of innocent people, but we have to start our own defense with a deep understanding that homeplaces have both personal and symbolic meaning. What we should work toward is the generous gesture: This place means everything to us! How can we preserve and share it? In a sense, political solutions might start with an emotional recreation of the suffering of the first generation.

Neglect of place has also had drastic consequences in the treatment of native people in America. Edward Casey (1993) describes the effects of forced resettlement on the Navajo people. The Navajo-Hopi Land Settlement Act of 1974 was meant to provide justice to both Navajo and Hopi peoples, but lawmakers did not consider the depth of attachment native peoples have for their land. The results of moving Navajos from their homes (even a very few miles) included an increase in premature deaths, alcoholism, suicide, and depression. For many Navajos, moving away from one's original location is equivalent to losing one's identity.

Expulsion from a homeplace is a major cause of the hatred that so often flares up between ethnic groups. Most scholars today discount the idea that the ethnic cleansings and genocide of the 20th century can be traced to ancient patterns of hatred (Kaufman 2002). Hatred more often arises within generational memory, and some of the most violent hatred is a direct result of displacing people from their homeplaces. Ethnic cleansing is often accompanied by attempts to erase all traces of the unwanted minority (Naimark 2002). The expelled are thus doubly wounded: not only are they separated from their homeplaces; their homeplaces are purged of their past presence and influence. In designing place-based education, we should be sensitive to the horrors that people inflict on others in tearing them from their roots and removing all traces of their prior existence.

ENVIRONMENTAL ASPECTS

There is broad agreement that the Earth needs our care. Everyone wants clean air, water, and productive soil, but we differ strongly on the urgency of environmental problems and even more on what solutions to try. No responsible system of education today ignores environmental topics, but curricula sometimes neglect the opposing arguments on sensitive issues. Too often we project the idea that all good people are on one side of a given issue; it follows that people on the other side are either bad or ignorant.

Because environmental issues are so complex, they provide a wonderful opportunity for critical thinking. As educators, we want young people to make a commitment to preservation of the natural world. However, a real commitment demands engagement, study, and critical thinking of the most difficult kind—thinking that examines and questions our own initial positions. David Naguib Pellow (2002) points out that even the best-intentioned environmentalists often make mistakes; they solve one problem only to encounter another that might have been avoided with foresight.

Young people are easily drawn to romantic and sentimental solutions. The so-called "tree-huggers" are right in wanting to preserve our forests, but they are wrong when they attack logging operations without considering how their proposed solutions may affect people and their livelihoods. If logging in a particular area must cease, how will the affected community survive economically? What are the best patterns of sustainable logging, and do they differ from one place to another?

Examples of environmental issues on which reasonable people differ abound, and students should be made aware of this. Are large dams always an ecological mistake? Is the development of nuclear energy environmentally destructive? Would drilling for oil in Alaska cause great ecological hardship? Are suggestions for alternative forms of energy feasible? Should deserts be made to bloom even if the cost is a huge consumption of water and eventual destruction of the desert's capacity to provide some sustenance for human life?[1] Should garbage be incinerated or dumped? Does the particular place where such endeavors are instituted matter?

Among the most important considerations in all of the above issues is the role of place. What does their place mean to people whose homes will be flooded by the construction of a dam? What are the risks to people in the vicinity of a nuclear facility? If incineration is a better method of waste disposal (is it?) than dumping, where should such facilities be located? Many critics (see Keller 1993; Pellow 2002) have pointed out that the poor suffer disproportionately from decisions involving place: they live in the valleys that are flooded, in the neighborhoods where incinerators and chemical plants are built, in the regions chosen for nuclear facilities and waste disposal. Thus another question for global citizens to ponder in considering solutions to environmental problems is, *Whose* place will be affected?

Sustainability is a keyword in today's environmental studies, and problems of sustainability differ across places. By "sustainable" we mean a method or way of life that can continue to support life and human activity indefinitely. Finding and maintaining sustainable methods of farming are directly related to place. Can places be transformed and controlled so that they will produce the highest possible yield of some product not natural to the area, or will such activity necessarily work against sustainability? Michael Pollan (2001) contrasts the Irish and Peruvian methods of potato farming. Attempting to produce large quantities of one kind of potato made Irish farms vulnerable to potato blight and led to the Great Famine. Peruvian farmers grow many different kinds of potatoes (as many as 3,000 kinds), each kind matched to the place (ecological niche) where it grows best. The Peruvian method is sustainable. A monoculture (the practice of devoting large expanses of farmland to just one crop) that forces a given place to produce heavily may not be sustainable. Often such a culture requires increasingly heavy doses of chemicals and pesticides. According to Pollan, even the chemical company Monsanto has acknowledged that "current agricultural technology is unsustainable" (2001, 191). Monsanto's answer, however, is not to match plants to places but to change plants through genetic engineering. Plant technologists have altered the potato's genes so that it will be inherently resistant to the Colorado potato beetle. We do not know what will happen when some of the new genes slip across species' lines. It would be a mistake at this stage either to condemn the new technology or to embrace it without qualification.

It is not only in agriculture that we seek sustainability. What makes a city or town sustainable? Urban ecologists and designers have studied many patterns in recent years, and students may be fascinated to learn that porches and large windows at the front of houses seem to deter crime. Similarly, alleys made attractive with artwork and partly inaccessible to motor vehicle traffic also make cities safer from crime (Ford 2000). In investigating their own cities, urban students should be invited to study urban patterns globally. There are beautiful old cities in many parts of the world. What gives them life? Why do others decay? What can we learn for our own cities? Part of global citizenship is a willingness to learn from one another.

Students need to examine suburbs, too. They might decide that the typical American suburb does not represent a sustainable way of life or, at least, that it can be sustained only at the cost of a reduced lifestyle for many non-suburban dwellers. The drawbacks of suburban living include increased needs for individual transportation, the separation of elderly and young from community activities, large lawns that may be ecologically damaging, and loss of habitat for wild creatures.

Another issue sure to arise in environmental education is the preservation of wilderness. Edward O. Wilson writes, "No question in environmental ethics cuts more deeply" (Wilson 2002, 143). Preservation of our large frontier forests—for example, the Amazon rain forest—is almost certainly essential for continued life on Earth, and organizations such as the Sierra Club, National Geographic, and The Nature Conservancy have presented a clear case for preservation. However, important as it is to preserve wilderness, commitment to that cause can induce a sense of complacency and self-righteousness in American and European young people. The areas to be preserved are far away (even within the United States), and it is easy to overlook the needs of people who may see financial survival in their development. Again, the issue is complex and requires a vigorous sense of global citizenship.

Concentration on vast stretches of wilderness may also blind us to the wonders of nature in our own backyards. Wilson is persuasive on this:

> The micro-wildernesses are more accessible than full-scale wildernesses. They are usually only minutes away, to be visited by microscope instead of jetliner. A simple tree in a park, harboring thousands of species, is an island, complete

with miniature mountains, valleys, lakes, and subterranean caverns. Scientists have only begun to explore these compacted worlds. Educators have made surprisingly little use of them in introducing the wonders of life to students. (Wilson 2002, 145)

CONNECTING THE LOCAL AND GLOBAL

There are two basic ways in which educators can help students connect local and global interests. One is to learn to care for our own local places, thus learning that commitment to the environment requires work—not just talk. Another is to study local places appreciatively and communicate something about them to the larger world. Communication is, of course, a two-way process: we can tell the story of our own place, and we can listen to the stories told by others of their places. Both are powerful learning strategies.

Wendell Berry (1995, 1996) has argued that care of the Earth begins with care of the places where we live and work. Obviously, as we saw in the paragraph above from Wilson, we can also learn much about the natural world by studying the plants and animals around us. It is the sort of study to which most children are attracted, and their fascination with the natural world can provide that stage of romance described by Alfred North Whitehead (1967) as the beginning of genuine learning.

Peter Kahn (1999) has shown that children need and appreciate a relationship to nature and that both their need and their understanding may grow developmentally. Gary Nabhan and Stephen Trimble (1994) also argue that children need wild places. Interestingly, however, the wild places advocated by these writers need not be vast wilderness places protected by national laws. There can be wild places in backyards, parks, empty lots, and schoolyards. As Wilson finds a whole region in one tree, children can find an exciting world under a few bushes.

These observations suggest that the project of global environmentalism might be significantly advanced by restoring the study of natural history in our schools. Such study takes place in the immediate surroundings of home and school. What wild creatures live in our area? Are they thriving? What plants are indigenous to the area? What can we do to preserve their lives and our connection to them?

Suburban students might make a serious study of their own and neighbors' backyards. Why do suburban homeowners put such great value on huge lawns? Lawns, as they are fed, watered, and mowed in suburbia, do not provide sustenance for valuable insects; they do not enrich the soil (as clover does, for example); and they take inordinate amounts of water, chemicals, and energy to keep them green and clipped. Sara Stein (1993) presents a charming study of lawns and their usurpation of land that might provide sustenance for native plants, birds, and all sorts of wild creatures. Giving up large lawns in favor of small ones surrounded by hedgerows, trees, and natural grasses would save time, money, and energy in addition to lives. Stein notes that there are few cows, horses, and sheep in suburbia to provide the lawnlike look of pastures:

> Lawns can no longer claim pastoral validity. They have outgrown it monstrously. Though now I understand why they need such care, I question why we give it. We spend $25 billion a year coddling this carpet that on an August day lies sprawled over 30 million acres of America, stupefied in the sun. (Stein 1993, 151)

Stein shows how beautiful, interesting, and life-sustaining alternatives can be.

Michael Pollan (1991) also describes the attractions of living in partly wild places. Our gardens are cultivated; they are not part of nature in the raw. Yet, as Pollan describes them, they constitute a *second nature*, a way of promoting the beauty and bounty of cultivated places and preserving a connection to wildness. How can we plan our vegetable and flower gardens so that they "fit" their natural surroundings? Which trees should we preserve? Where should we place water in the garden?

And what better place than a garden is there to study insect life? Too many children today are taught to be terrified of insects and spiders. This is a great shame, for many insects are both fascinating and useful. Indeed, with the help of several splendid books, my husband and I have grown beautiful and delicious vegetables on the New Jersey shore (in view of the Atlantic Ocean) without pesticides. A need may arise—one can never be sure about these things—but so far, variety in plantings and the care to preserve and welcome helpful insects have worked.

This past summer we found large green caterpillars on our parsley. They were actually quite lovely—green with black and yellow spots. We plucked them off carefully and put each one in a jar with several branches of moist parsley. I cleaned their jars every day. We watched them spin their cocoons, and in about three weeks, gorgeous butterflies—black swallowtails— emerged. This was a wonderful experience for us and for all of our summer visitors, and it saved the parsley, because I could cut individual stems and prevent the stripping that loose caterpillars do. Children should learn about the lives of insects and how the presence of some is desirable in our gardens (Grissell 2001).

A second way to connect the local and global is to encourage students to study their locality appreciatively and then tell its stories in language accepted as standard by the wider society. An outstanding example of this approach is the *Foxfire* series, the first of which (Wigginton 1968) describes a way in which to stay with the local and, at the same time, to transcend it.

Students in an Appalachian community were encouraged to go into the hills to interview residents about all sorts of things: planting time, ghost stories, poetry, songs, crafts, food, and even moonshining. Kids who had been completely indifferent to a standard English course became excited about starting their own magazine, and the effort resulted in multiple volumes of well-written mountain lore. Not only did the students find pride in their locality, but they also learned to use the standard English they had previously resisted. They wanted to tell the world about their part of Appalachia. Their work is so powerful—so filled with common sense, beauty, and charm—that just mentioning it tends to distract me from my own writing. I want to read their work again.

Surely such an approach can be tried anywhere. Basically, it is a way of motivating students to appreciate their own region and to learn standard English. Appreciation and criticism go hand in hand, and such study can provide the foundation for a wider and more intelligent global environmentalism. At the same time, learning standard English is, of course, a means toward fuller participation in the larger society.

It is hoped that as students study and write about their own homeplaces, they will become receptive to the stories of people in other places. Themes of place can be found in novels, poetry, biography, and essays. Many works containing these themes are regularly assigned in schools, but the themes of place are often ignored in favor of tedious discussions of vocabulary, metaphor, and technique.

Who, once having read it without rush or coercion, could forget Hardy's depiction (n.d., 33) of an old man cackling and dancing with the help of his cane (a three-legged jig) around the furze fire on the heath? Later in the same book, we encounter a lesson in real happiness when Clym, with appreciation, returns from a wider world of success to the heath: "Take all the varying hates felt by Eustacia Vye towards the heath, and translate them into loves, and you have the heart of Clym" (Hardy n.d., 199). Too often, we force such novels whole on teenagers, when we might instead read excerpts to them, enticing and inviting them. Invited, they might even want to read some of Hardy's poetry, which is filled with a love of place. What is wonderful about this way of recognizing place is that it connects so naturally to a host of other themes. In Hardy, we have an opportunity to discuss happiness versus material success, religion, intellectual snobbery, the passions and tragedies of love, betrayal, and faithfulness.

In addition to the many stories of particular places and their influence on the individuals living there, we can move the discussion up a notch in abstraction and study the ways in which people have cared for or destroyed the immediate world around them. There are many, many books available today that describe the attachment of Native Americans to their land (Basso 1996; Casey 1993) and, in contrast, histories of human greed that tends to destroy the very places that some love (Reisner 1993). Students should learn, too, that love and greed can be found in the same people. Highly romantic stories rarely tell the complete truth.

The theme discussed earlier—finding wilderness in our own backyards—is repeated in literature. John Elder (1998) points out that "Robert Frost valued wildness at the *edge* and even in the *midst* of civilization" (Elder 1998, 22). Further, Elder writes:

> Thoreau loved the wetlands and other "unproductive" areas not apart from but in relation to the cultivated lands, as revitalizing elements for entire regions. Growing up in the Bay Area, I relished occasional car trips into the vastness and beauty of the Sierra Nevada. But as a householder in Vermont, I love even more the tattered, recovering wilderness just outside our back door, where in every season our family can ramble among the crags that overhang our roof and that frame the playing fields of the children's schools. (ibid., 22)

HUMAN FLOURISHING AND PLACE

I have already more than hinted at the importance of place in the lives of individuals and groups. Global citizenship demands an understanding and sympathy for people's attachment to place. One way to encourage this understanding, as we have seen, is to include natural history in the curriculum so that, at least, appreciation is developed for one's own natural surroundings. John Dewey (1916) made a strong argument for the study of natural history as an integral part of geography:

> To include nature study within geography doubtless seems forced; verbally, it is. But in educational idea there is but one reality . . . Nature and the earth should be equivalent terms, and so should earth study and nature study. (Dewey 1916, 213)

Dewey sees the need to integrate geography, history, and nature study, for human events occur in particular times and places. Speaking of economics and industrial history, he writes:

> When the history of work, when the conditions of using the soil, forest, mine, of domesticating and cultivating grains and animals, of manufacture and distribution, are left out of account, history tends to become merely literary—a systemized romance of a mythical humanity living upon itself instead of upon the earth. (Dewey 1916, 216)

The tendency to tell the story of a "mythical humanity" can be found in almost any contemporary secondary school American history text. We have overcome the older practice of leaving out nonwhite cultural groups, and authors are compelled to include at least a few women in their texts. How-ever, the fierce political battles over land, water, and other natural resources are often omitted. In a popular text of more than 1,000 pages, there is only one reference (in the index) to dams, and yet the benefits and harms of these structures figure prominently in the real history and future of the United States. In one section, the text speaks romantically of the hardships of pio-neers in the American West, declaring that—despite the dangers and diffi-culties—most stayed. In a later section, the text admits that "thousands" migrated from the Dust Bowl in the 1930s. A more accurate and vivid story would mention that the population of Hall County, Texas, dropped from 40,000 to 1,000, and that the Dakotas lost "at least 146,000 people" (Reisner 1993, 151). Further, the Dust Bowl phenomenon would not be discussed as a "natural disaster" but as a human-made catastrophe that is likely to be repeated sometime in the current century.

Part of the blame for such catastrophes falls on ignorance—simply not knowing what agricultural practices are sustainable in a given place—but much of it can be attributed to greed and deceptive political maneuvers. The real history of the American West is filled with stories of political rivalries and competition for projects that did not serve the common interest: irrigat-ing high-elevation farms that could never repay even the price of the water, flooding good farmland to build reservoirs, robbing small farmers of water to supply large farmers, protecting small white towns while allowing Indian farms to be flooded, ruthlessly grabbing water resources from our Canadian and Mexican neighbors (see Reisner 1993).

Texts and teachers should tell a balanced story. Not all reclamation projects have been motivated by greed, and some have accomplished near miracles by supplying hydroelectric power, controlling floods, and irrigat-ing fertile fields. Reisner (1993), for example, acknowledges that the great dams of the West were instrumental in winning World War II. The power generated by these dams made the United States the world's most produc-tive industrial nation. Neglecting positive results would be a mistake. It would reproduce the errors discussed earlier in our account of environmental ro-manticism. The problems are complex and require complex solutions, but solutions are unlikely to be found unless our young people become global citizens in the truest sense. They have to care about their homeplaces and those of others, and they have to care enough to engage in serious study of both natural and political problems.

Study of environmental problems in the United States—especially man-agement of water—could also help students to understand what is going on in other parts of the world and why so many people are now protesting against the projects of the International Monetary Fund and World Bank (Bigelow and Peterson 2002; Stiglitz 2002). People in many parts of the world are fighting to keep their lands from being flooded and their forests from destruction. In doing so, are they thoughtlessly depriving themselves of the benefits of industrialization? Can compromises be found that will lead to both sustainable agriculture and sustainable urban life?

Attention to place can serve an integrating function in school studies. The connection to peace studies and the sociology of poverty is obvious. When people flourish, they flourish in places. Driving people from their homes or homeplaces is an act that reverberates in hatred and despair. Still, people who are well rooted sometimes fail to flourish. Poverty, too, sits in places (Duncan 1999). In studying poverty, however, we must be careful not to equate financial poverty with poverty of spirit. If people need to or want to improve their financial condition, can they be helped to do so without destroying or abandoning the places they love? E. V. Walter (1988) suggests a holistic sociology of people and places to get a better picture of what financial hardship means in individual lives.

Place should figure prominently in discussion of globalization. Joseph Stiglitz (2002) points out that although it is officially committed to eliminating poverty worldwide, the World Bank often exercises strategies that make things worse for the world's poorest. He writes:

> The question has to do with the impact of *particular policies*. Some policies promote growth but have little effect on poverty; some promote growth but actually increase poverty; and some promote growth and reduce poverty at the same time. (Stiglitz 2002, 82)

These last strategies are those Stiglitz says should be sought. But I would add that we must look beyond growth and financial poverty. A more holistic examination might reveal that small financial gains cannot compensate for damage to or loss of place.

Place is a powerful theme in peace studies, sociology, history, and literature. It is also powerful in science and biography. Students learn in biology classes how much of Darwin's theory of natural selection came out of his exploration of the Galapagos, but few hear about the importance of his home, Down House, in Downe Village, Kent, England. Very much attached to his home and region, Darwin did all of his writing and much of his later experimentation at home (Browne 2002). Just as place was central in the lives of creatures he studied, it was central in Darwin's life.

Finally, in considering the importance of place on human flourishing, we should return to the role of place in human happiness (Noddings 2003a). Many people love their homeplaces and derive great joy from them. Walter quotes Aristophanes on this: "What a powerful thing one's love for a place can be!" (Walter 1988, 146). As noted earlier, we find this theme again and again in literature, but we rarely find it emphasized in schools. Perhaps, as Walter suggests, the theme is alien to modernity. In his appreciative critique

of Freud, Walter notes that for Freud the mind seemed to comprise its own
territory or place:

> Patients searching for an identity express the old question asked by Oedipus,
> "Who am I?" but the next Oedipal question, "*Where* do I belong?" does not
> find any ground in psychoanalytic theory, which constructs the mind as its own
> place. (Walter 1988, 112)

The second Oedipal question belongs in schools, and it should belong to any
thorough consideration of global education.

NOTE

1. This topic is explored in a compelling way in Wallace Stegner's biography
of John Wesley Powell, *Beyond the Hundredth Meridian: John Wesley Powell and
the Second Opening of the West* (New York: Penguin Books, 1992. Original work
published 1954).

CHAPTER 4

Differing Concepts of Citizenship: Schools and Communities as Sites of Civic Development

Gloria Ladson-Billings

ACCORDING TO TALCOTT PARSONS, the concept of citizenship is based on full membership in the "societal community" (Parsons 1965). And in his 1964 classic, *Class, Citizenship, and Social Development*, T. H. Marshall asserted that citizenship in the nation-state involves three components: the civil (or legal), the political, and the social. According to Marshall, the civil or legal component of citizenship evolves first and involves the security of each individual and property, as well as individual freedoms such as speech, religion, assembly and association, and equality before the law. "These rights take precedence over any particular political status or interest and over any social component such as wealth or poverty, prominence or obscurity" (Parsons 1965, 1017).

The political aspect of citizenship refers to the ability to participate in collective goal attainment at the societal level, through the process of government. Although most citizens are neither functionaries of the government nor wholly controlled government subjects, they do have rights of participation in governmental processes through the franchise and through the exercise of fundamental rights that may influence policy. Thus, citizens are able to assemble, lobby, petition, and protest to make their voices heard. In the United States, the political party system is a primary way to influence the government.

The societal component of citizenship refers to an ability to have access to the society's resources and capacities that permit social mobility and comfort. Access to health care, education, employment opportunities, and non-discriminatory housing are examples of the benefits that societal citizenship offers. These three components of citizenship are good indicators of the degree to which some members of the U.S. society fail to be acknowledged as full citizens.

In delineating the components of citizenship in the nation-state and arguing that various racial groups have differential access to citizenship, Parsons suggested that securing the social component was the only obstacle to full citizenship for people of color. Although, as a mid-1960s thesis, Parsons focused on African Americans, his argument clearly can be extended to Latinos, American Indians, Asian/Pacific Islanders, and others considered nonwhites. However, scholars like Renato Rosaldo and Will Kymlicka have since advanced alternate conceptions of citizenship. Rosaldo states that "One needs to distinguish the formal level of theoretical universality (of citizenship) from the substantive level of exclusionary and marginalizing practices" (1997, 27).[1] Kymlicka (1995) points out that liberal democracy and ethnic or minority group rights need not be antithetical. For these scholars and others, the meaning of citizenship in a global context that Parsons failed to address remains part of the unfinished agenda of civic education.

MAKING DEMOCRATS IN UNDEMOCRATIC SPACES

Anthropologists might argue that all education is citizenship education, since every society works to socialize its youth into the prevailing social system (Spindler 1987). Indeed, we attempt to teach our children to be like us. Such a system works when we guarantee young people that their participation in the educational system will have a promised payoff, for example, they will be accorded the full rights and privileges of citizenship. However, in societies that have strict differences in status based on race, class, and gender, not all students accept the pronouncement that they can have access to full citizenship through education.

Terrie Epstein (2001) and Catherine Cornbleth (2002) have described the sense of alienation and anger many students of color feel toward the nation and their place in it. Epstein's research suggests that even when students of different racial or ethnic groups are sitting in the same classrooms, their perspectives about the veracity and reliability of what U.S. history and citizenship mean can differ widely. Why is it that citizenship education has different meanings for different groups of students and remains problematic for most students? Kathleen Cotton's review of the citizenship education literature identifies 12 major criticisms of civic education (Cotton 1996). Those criticisms are briefly summarized here:

1. *A lack of meaningful content.* Most students experience civic education as a set of facts separated from any meaningful context. They

are asked to memorize the Bill of Rights but are rarely asked to understand what those rights mean in everyday life.

2. *Irrelevance.* Rarely do students experience content connected to their own life experiences. A typical adolescent response of "why do we have to learn this?" often receives a response that says, "You're going to need this someday."

3. *A lack of focus on citizen rights.* Rather than helping students understand that citizenship guarantees tolerance for the expression of guaranteed freedom, most civic education focuses on compliance with laws.

4. *A lack of training in thinking and process skills.* Although discussions of curriculum urge teachers to foster critical thinking, problem-solving, and decision-making, few school-based civic education programs reinforce such skills.

5. *Focus on passive learning.* Typical civic education courses are organized and taught using lectures, textbooks, and pencil-and-paper exams.

6. *Avoidance of controversial topics.* Few teachers are willing to take up the social controversies that arise in a democratic society. Rather than discuss pros and cons of the nation's policies, both domestic and international, most teachers stick to comfortable and official discourses about the virtues of the nation.

7. *Focus on teacher control and student obedience.* Rather than foster democratic behaviors that emerge from independent thinking and social action, civic education employs a language of control and compliance.

8. *Low-quality curriculum for low-track students.* Lower-track students who often are cynical about the prospects of democratic citizenship are more often exposed to antidemocratic, authoritarian pedagogy and vacuous curriculum. Low-track students are more often asked to memorize the documents of democracy rather than understand and act on them.

9. *A lack of attention to global issues.* Rarely does civic education in the United States explore the role the nation plays in the wider global context. Few civics curricula address international law and the concept of global citizenship.

10. *Limited and shallow textbook content.* The major civic issues of our history and current situation are poorly represented in textbook content. Constitutional crises such as presidential impeachment, controversial Supreme Court decisions (or upcoming rulings), or legislation are either not addressed or treated in superficial ways.

11. *Text-bound instruction.* Despite the poor quality of texts, most teachers rely on them as the major source of instruction.

12. *Inappropriate assessment.* Few authentic assessments of citizenship are offered in civic education. Instead, civic education is dominated by the use of standardized tests to assess learning, and letter grades serve as a proxy for student learning.

The paradox of attempting to use passive, irrelevant, noncontroversial curriculum and instruction to prepare students for active citizenship in a democratic and multicultural society is startling. How can we do a better job of preparing citizens? Why is reliance on passivity and compliance so prevalent? Why does American society accept this kind of civic education?

NEW CITIZENS—DOWNSIZED, CORPORATE, CULTURAL, AND FLEXIBLE

Crenson and Ginsberg (2002) argue that our current government does not want active citizens and detail the change in citizen action over time. In the 19th century, America was regarded as an exceptional country because of the vitality of its democratic institutions. The various political parties were sites of democratic activity and debate. Citizens who wanted change, particularly those with ready access to the franchise, mobilized as groups to exert pressure on Congress and turned out to vote in large numbers. This relationship between government and its citizens was reciprocal. Active citizens were excellent candidates to staff public agencies and serve in the armed services. However, as the 20th century came to an end, American democracy had radically changed.

In less than 100 years, the economic pressures of our highly technological society had forced citizens to concentrate more on their own well-being and less on a notion of the public good. The need for at least two incomes to maintain middle-class households, which required that citizens work further away from their home communities, left less time for civic participation. Instead, middle-income citizens directed their energies toward maintaining their households and allowing private entities to supplant public services, leaving public services for lower- to working-class citizens. For example, public health, public transportation, and public housing in many cities are strictly the domain of poor people. Unfortunately, public schools in major urban centers are beginning to reflect this same trend.

The emphasis on *homo economicus* moved the society from one made up of public citizens to one dominated by corporate citizens. The good citizen became the one who contributed to an expanding economy. The most despised citizen was the one who relied on public monies for basic needs. Crenson and Ginsberg suggest that so thoroughly has American democracy become consumer-driven that in the aftermath of the horrors of the September 11th terrorist attacks on the World Trade Center and the Pentagon, President George W. Bush urged citizens to help the nation by shopping and traveling (Crenson and Ginsberg 2002). Within days, companies like McDonald's and General Motors were filling their television ads with patriotic symbols and appealing to a frightened citizenry with words about spending for America. Instead of seeing ourselves as citizens, we are encouraged by our governmental leaders to think of ourselves as consumers.

Rosaldo (1997) introduces the notion of "cultural citizenship" to suggest that two concepts—culture and citizenship—thought to be competing can actually be merged in complementary ways. In the case of Latinos, he suggests that a deep and abiding commitment to home cultures, languages, and customs need not interfere with one's commitment to the body politic. Kymlicka (1995) argues that the dynamic of the modern (or perhaps postmodern) nation-state makes the notion of singular civic identities untenable. Instead of casting citizenship as an "either/or" proposition (i.e., one is either a citizen of the United States or a citizen of Mexico), we can come to think of today's citizens as "both/and" (i.e., one might be both a citizen of the United States and have cultural, political, and historical allegiances to another nation or cultural group simultaneously). These multiple civic identities play out across individual and group roles and activities. People are both individuals entitled to citizen rights that may be accessed whenever necessary, and members of groups who may mobilize to secure rights and privileges because of that group membership. For example, when Rosa Parks courageously sat in an empty seat in the front of a Montgomery, Alabama, public bus, she was asserting her individual right as a citizen to have fair and equal access to the available public transportation. But when the African-American community in Montgomery joined together to boycott the buses, they were functioning as a group to secure rights for everyone.

Individuals move back and forth across many identities, and the way the society responds to these identities either binds people to or alienates them from the civic culture. The degree to which the broader society embraces and accepts multiple identities reflects the degree to which individuals see themselves as citizens. In our post-September 11th environment, individuals with identities as Muslim or "Middle Eastern" have had their loyalty and allegiance to America called into question. Indeed, in the 1960 election, John F. Kennedy, the first viable Catholic candidate, was questioned as to his loyalty to the United States versus his loyalty to the Vatican.

As we consider multicultural citizenship we must note the unequal power relations that exist between and among various ethnic, racial, and cultural groups. In most instances where the multicultural nation-state examines the relations between whites and people of color, whites are in the dominant position and maintain the economic, social, political, and cultural advantages (Delgado 1995). These advantages allow an almost seamless melding of the cultural and the civic for the dominant group. For example, in the United States, whites have the luxury of substituting their cultural identities for an "American" identity while simultaneously being viewed as more loyal, more patriotic, and more committed to the nation-state. U.S. citizens of color frequently are accused of being ethnocentric and less patriotic (Wilkins 2001). This characterization seems curious given the identity politics many ethnic groups—Irish Americans, Italian Americans, Jewish Americans—historically have engaged in to consolidate their political and electoral power (Kilson 1998). Kymlicka asserts, "If there is a viable way to promote a sense of solidarity and common purpose in a multination state, it will involve accommodating, rather than subordinating, national identities. People from different national groups will only share an allegiance to the larger polity if they see it as the context within which their national identity is nurtured rather than subordinated" (Kymlicka 1998, 182).

Ong (1999) offers a more complicated view of citizenship when she argues that global capitalism, international travel, communication, and mass media have created a new kind of citizen. Instead of being bound by geopolitical boundaries and national loyalties, people are developing multiple allegiances that transform them into "flexible citizens." Such citizens, according to Ong, are more committed to their work and careers than to any particular national identity. These individuals chase work wherever it may be and threaten long-standing notions of what it means to be a citizen. She is careful, however, to differentiate between diasporas and cosmopolitanisms. Diasporas are comprised of marginalized, displaced, and victimized subjects trying to make a place for themselves in the modern world, while cosmopolitans are worldly, progressive intellectuals who *decide* to be global citizens.

All four versions of citizenship—downsized, corporate, cultural, and flexible—are available to students in our schools. And yet the need for young people to work harder than those in previous generations to maintain a minimal standard of living means that fewer and fewer of them have an opportunity to engage in civic participation. Those who have an opportunity for postsecondary training become an important demographic for consumer goods and credit. The regular and predictable failure and underachievement of various ethnic and racial groups creates citizens who bind themselves to cultural identities in opposition to national allegiances. What guidance are we offering within our schools to help young Americans develop their identities as local and global citizens?

WHO DOES THE SCHOOL THINK YOU ARE?

The social studies curriculum in U.S. schools is designed to prepare students for active citizenship. However, this preparation is likely to be in the form of uncritical acceptance of the United States as the "best" country in the world. Such preparation tends to foster ethnocentrism and nationalism. In the 1988 *California History–Social Science Framework* (State Department of Education, 1988) teachers are told: "The younger generation needs to understand our history, our institutions, our ideals, our values, our economy, and our relations with other nations in the world." Thus the major focus is on American life with a passing reference to the "rest of the world."

Too often, official curricula treat all students as if they were white, middle-class, natural-born citizens. Thus the idea that some students may feel conflicts about their place in the United States rarely surfaces. Students who have family and cultural ties to Mexico, Cuba, other parts of Latin America, Southeast Asia, and Africa may struggle with the recruitment into a U.S. national discourse. Allendoefer (2001) points out that more recent immigrants often work hard to maintain an identity associated with their native land. In her study of Vietnamese immigrant teenagers she found that students resisted being categorized as "Asian Americans" and reported no affinity toward Chinese, Japanese, or Filipino youths in their schools. Of course, the school assumed a monolithic "Asian" identity that would quickly become an "Asian-American" identity.

Not only does the school curriculum often assume a white identity for all students, it also assumes a middle-income identity. Such assumptions mean that the challenges of poverty—economic uncertainty, limited resources, limited access to generational wealth (e.g., property, education, assets)—are ignored as teachers attempt to assign homework tasks and involve parents in the day-to-day lives of students. Increasingly, the costs associated with attending public school are beginning to rival private schools. Notebooks, pencils, art supplies, computer disks, physical education supplies, calculators, and field trip fees are a few of the costs families are asked to bear. Children whose families are unable to cover these costs soon come to feel that they are less than citizens. Schools assume that the work that students do before or after school (paper routes, fast food workers, babysitters, etc.) is optional and treat the income from such work as "extra" money—to purchase a car, to buy special clothing, to finance luxuries. However, data from the National Center for Children in Poverty (2002) indicate that 37 percent of American children live in low-income families, 16 percent live in poverty, the U.S. child poverty rate is substantially higher than that of most other major western industrialized nations, and the child poverty rate is highest for African-American and Latino children. United States schools also assume that its students are native English speakers. Despite the fact that the 2000 census indicates that Latinos are the largest group of people of color, most school curricula ignore the linguistic diversity that teachers and schools confront. Civic documents and speeches that frame the national character (the Declaration of Independence, the Constitution, the *Federalist Papers*, the Gettysburg

Address) almost always are presented in English. We know little of how translations of these documents impact their meanings and how much is lost when a second language learner attempts to understand them. We also fail to recognize that preparation for global citizenship should entail multilingualism. Too little in our current civic education addresses the diversity that is a part of most urban schools, and increasingly a part of suburban and rural schools. Curriculum developers seem to believe that our students are all white, all middle-class, and all native English speakers.

Insofar as our curricula frame concepts of citizenship, schools struggle with the notion of developing global citizens because of the limited view of citizenship that they offer to students. According to Andrzejewski and Alessio (1999), school-based citizenship education has a heavy focus on compliance. Even at the college level, they argue, students believe that good citizenship entails voting, obeying the law, paying taxes, saluting the flag, and saying the Pledge of Allegiance. These limited constructions of citizenship, combined with the absence of diversity awareness, do not help students take on the more challenging role of global citizenship. Thus, it is more likely that such work will occur in alternative settings.

ARE THERE ALTERNATE CHOICES FOR DEVELOPING CITIZENS?

As we examine the weaknesses in current civic education from Cotton's research, it is clear that schools generally fall short of meeting their civic responsibility. However, some programs are working to enlist young people into civic participation activities. The most often cited form of youth civic participation is volunteer work. According to the Center for Information and Research in Civic Learning (CIRCLE 2002), 72 percent of young adults say they have donated money, clothes, or food to a community or church group; 49 percent see volunteering for community activities as most important versus 12 percent for participating in politics and government; 37 percent never volunteer; 33 percent who grew up with political discussion in their home volunteer at least once a month; and 30 percent volunteer because they were asked to by a church or a person. In its 2003 report *The Civic Mission of Schools*, the Carnegie Corporation and CIRCLE assert that school is the appropriate and best place to develop citizens. However, I would argue that the concept of the role of the citizen advanced by the report fails to acknowledge a global dimension to citizenship. The report suggests that competent and responsible citizens . . .

1. *Are informed and thoughtful.* They have a grasp and an appreciation of history and the fundamental processes of American democracy; an understanding of public and community issues; an ability

      to obtain information when needed; a capacity to think critically; and a willingness to enter into dialogue with others about different points of view and to understand diverse perspectives. They are tolerant of ambiguity and resist simplistic answers to complex questions.

2. *Participate in their communities.* They belong to and contribute to groups in civil society that offer venues for Americans to participate in public service, work together to overcome problems, and pursue an array of cultural, social, political, and religious interests and beliefs.

3. *Act politically.* They have the skills, knowledge, and commitment needed to accomplish public purposes—for instance, by organizing people to address social issues, solving problems in groups, speaking in public, petitioning and protesting to influence public policy, and voting.

4. *Have moral and civic virtues.* They are concerned for the rights and welfare of others, socially responsible, willing to listen to alternate perspectives, confident in their capacity to make a difference, and ready to contribute personally to civic and political action. They strike a reasonable balance between their own interests and the common good. They recognize the importance of and practice civic duties such as voting and respecting the rule of law.

                (Carnegie Corporation and CIRCLE 2003, 10)

But will citizens with these skills be equipped to make judgments and decisions about the nation's foreign policy and international relations?

    Despite the increased emphasis on civic learning and participation in schools, we must often look beyond school in order to find opportunities for students to develop competencies of citizenship, especially global citizenship. For many students, religious affiliations provide a vehicle for volunteerism and international understanding. Under the rubric of our common humanity, religious groups often establish missions that extend beyond national boundaries. For other students, international political activist organizations provide an opportunity to participate in the global community. Organizations such as Greenpeace, Amnesty International, and the World Social Forum focus on world conditions. For students of color, groups such as the World Council of Indigenous Peoples, First Nations Congress, Pan-African Congress, Southern Poverty Law Center, and the Children's Defense Fund provide both international and national opportunities for civic action.

    Typical school programs—traditional and alternative—tend to focus on local community service. In January 2003, National Public Radio broadcast a series entitled "The Citizen Student." The third broadcast in the series, *Civic Lessons Beyond the Classroom*, looked at the variety of volunteer programs students are offered. One glaring failure of such programs is that they do not translate into student interest and activism in creating government solutions to current problems. Students are recruited to collect canned goods for the hungry without discussion and guidance about why hunger continues to exist in a country with a surplus of food. Or, as reported on the NPR broadcast, schools sponsor parties for children at a local homeless shelter but do not help their students understand why there is a shortage of affordable housing.

In the final broadcast in the NPR series, *Teaching Patriotism in Time of War*, we hear from two classroom teachers with very different approaches to civic education. One teacher attempts to help his students critically examine what it means to be a citizen and raise questions about what the government does in citizens' names. The other teacher strongly believes that the September 11th terrorist attack means that teachers must teach strict loyalty and support of the nation. Clearly, the matter of citizenship is complicated and the messages delivered in schools often mixed.

One of the challenges schools experience in fostering active citizenship is the inactive citizenship of many of the adults who surround students. Teachers, administrators, parents, and adult community members often fail to exhibit the kind of civic engagement that models active citizenship for students. Vincent Harding relates the words of a young man who addresses the needs of young people in a democratic society. "What we need are signposts to help us find the way. I don't mean no regular signposts . . . I mean like live, human signposts, people—people we can look at, be with, listen to . . . That's what we need. Signposts" (Harding 1990, 15).

While students may crave those human signposts, the increased personal scrutiny that elected officials and political hopefuls experience discourages many citizens from entering public life. Instances of corruption and corporate greed foster cynicism among the general electorate and, specifically, among young people. During an accreditation visit to a high school in an urban school district the evaluators noticed that the inside covers of the students' American Government textbooks were defaced. The inside covers contained words from the Preamble and the Bill of Rights. Students had marked them out and scribbled the words "Lies, lies, lies" over them. The students' anger at what can only be seen as the nation's broken promises to them was palpable. What kind of civic learning needs to go on in this environment? How can we convince students who have little or no access to the social benefits that Parsons claims are available to every citizen to become active and productive citizens? Similarly, how do we help students who, although they enjoy society's benefits, believe that their only responsibility is to earn enough money, prestige, and status to influence power brokers to champion their interests above all others?

CONCLUSION

I am convinced that until students begin to see democracy work in their own local communities, their ability to work for it as a part of the common good and a worthwhile global strategy is unlikely to materialize. One of the best examples of this strategy is exemplified in the work and legacy of Myles Horton, founder of the Highlander Folk School, which began as a center of training for union organizers. Horton understood that "the people with the problems are also the people with the solutions" (Ayers 1998, 153). This philosophy prompted Horton to create the only free space where labor organizers, civil rights activists, antipoverty workers, and other community workers assembled to solve local (and ultimately national) problems. In the 1950s, Highlander Folk School was the only place in the South where white and African-American citizens lived and worked together to test the strength of a Constitution that declared that we are all created equal. Some of Highlander's "graduates" included Eleanor Roosevelt, Pete Seeger, Woody Guthrie, Martin Luther King Jr., Rosa Parks, Andrew Young, Fannie Lou Hamer, Esau Jenkins, and Septima Clark. These individuals represent the best of American civic values. They understand the way our local problems and solutions can have global impact.

One of the more tangible examples of the way local solutions have global impact was demonstrated in Bejing's Tiananmen Square. As the young people demonstrated for freedom there were banners and t-shirts with the words "We Shall Overcome!," the same words of the African-American freedom movement. One of the Chinese students declared, "We are willing to starve for democracy." Harding (1990) points to the similarity of the statement of African-American nonviolent activist C. T. Vivian, who is captured on film in the awardwinning *Eyes on the Prize* video shouting to the white sheriff in Selma, Alabama, "We are willing to be beaten for democracy. And you misuse democracy in the streets. You beat people blind in order that they will not have the privilege to vote."

As the image from Tiananmen Square suggests, the U.S. local struggle became the template for a global one. In an interview with a Chinese student in Shanghai just before the Tiananmen Square showdown, the student said the only thing the Chinese students and intellectuals wanted from the United States was its "advanced technology." Then she was asked whether or not there were any American ideas that interested them, like democracy. The student responded, "Yes, but only if they are *advanced ideas* about democracy" (Harding 1990, 33). The students had already read about the American Revolution, George Washington, Thomas Jefferson, James Madison, and the other founding fathers. They were craving information and help with the real test of democracy—the fight for civil rights in the face of professed commitments (as well as documents and laws) to democracy. Such advanced ideas can only come in via deep understanding of the fight for freedom. The *Brown v. Board of Education of Topeka* decision, the Montgomery Bus Boycott, the sit-ins and Freedom Rides, the Mississippi Freedom Summer and the rise of the Mississippi Freedom Democratic Party, Dr. King's 1960 Chicago campaign, the Poor People's Campaign, the struggle for Black studies and Black education, Native Rights, and Language Rights all exemplify advanced ideas about democracy that might inform the process of developing a consciousness of global citizenship. Until we can assure our own young people that they will have an opportunity to move toward advanced ideas about democracy, we cannot hope for their engagement in the public good, locally or globally.

NOTE

1. While beyond the scope of this chapter, the history of the United States clearly indicates that the criteria for citizenship in the nation's early years were based on race, gender, and class.

CHAPTER 5

Incorporating Internationalism into the Social Studies Curriculum

Stephen J. Thornton

CITIZENSHIP EDUCATION HAS ALWAYS been a hallmark of American public education. Americans now live, however, in a world in which vital civic concerns routinely cross national boundaries. Global interdependence means that we really don't have a choice whether to educate for internationalism, a policy or practice of cooperation among nations. In this chapter I suggest that there have been and are substantial obstacles to teaching internationalism in American schools. Nevertheless, significant opportunities for teaching *about* internationalism, perhaps even teaching *for* internationalism, exist in the standard high school social studies curriculum. Since introducing new courses is an uncertain venture, I suggest alternative methods and provide illustrative topics for integrating internationalism into the current curriculum. Peacekeeping, economics, and the environment are suggested as particularly important topics for internationalism. An extended example of national self-determination and ethnic cleansing in 20th-century eastern and central Europe are presented. I conclude that greater attention to internationalism in the curriculum will depend on the provision of models from curriculum leaders and the exercise of educational imagination on the part of teachers.

George Washington, John Adams, Thomas Jefferson, and Benjamin Franklin, among other founders of the American form of republican government, recognized that an informed citizenry was essential to its survival. Thus, from the beginning, there has always been a linkage in the United States between the rights and duties of national citizenship and public education. Over the more than two centuries since U.S. independence, however, the world's nations have grown markedly more interdependent; for good or ill, Americans now live in a world in which vital civic concerns routinely cross national boundaries. Although Americans have in the past sometimes hoped that ignoring the world would insulate them from it, if this was ever possible the day has passed.

Global interdependence requires that Americans acquire relevant knowledge and a receptive attitude about internationalism, a policy or practice of cooperation among nations on matters such as peacekeeping, economics, and the environment. Although educating for internationalism often seeks to eliminate exploitation, militarism, and national vainglory, it is nonetheless reconcilable with a reasoned loyalty to a nation-state (Glendon 2001; Marsden 2000; Schlesinger 1938). Internationalism may include the study of problems such as destruction of forests and wildlife habitats, the effects of which do not respect national boundaries, thus underscoring global ecological interdependence and compelling some degree of cross-national cooperation (Weidensaul 1999).

This chapter concerns internationalist perspectives in U.S. high school social studies curricula. By "curriculum" I mean more than a group or series of topics on internationalism (Eisner 1972). A curriculum is a series of activities designed to engage the student in some content that is intended to have educational consequences. It must also engage the student in some type of activity, such as discussing peacekeeping in the former Yugoslavia, graphing economic growth in the Baltic republics, or observing photographs of desertification in West Africa. As these examples of activities imply, I am restricting my comments to social studies, which I define by its customary American usage as that part of the curriculum devoted to social questions such as family life, politics, and economics, and war and peace (Dewey 1969).

Although the U.S. education system is decentralized to a degree uncommon among industrialized nations, a de facto national social studies curriculum exists. It is evident, for instance, in textbook series and to some degree in the course scope and sequence of required social studies courses in the 50 states and the District of Columbia (D.C.). Customarily these courses include subject matters such as U.S. history, civics and problems of democracy, world geography, history and cultures, economics, and current events. For example, although it requires a full four years of social studies and is not necessarily typical in content, New York State's scope and sequence captures the spirit of most high school social studies programs in the other 49 states and D.C.:

Grade 9: Global history and geography
Grade 10: Global history and geography
Grade 11: United States history and government
Grade 12: Participation in government (one semester) and economics
        and economic decisionmaking (one semester)
                    (New York State Education Department 1990s)

Overall, in this chapter I first point out why alternatives to modal so-cial studies curricular arrangements such as these may not be the most effec-tive means of promoting the teaching of internationalism. While curricula designed directly to teach internationalism promise thorough treatment, this approach often confronts significant resistance when it comes to dissemina-tion and implementation. Thus, although approaching internationalism through standard courses runs the risk of its educational purposes being swallowed up by established curricular emphases, with vigilance this need not be an insurmountable obstacle to its substantial treatment. Teaching *about* internationalism has long been common in the standard curriculum and seldom evokes controversy. The admittedly more ambitious and possi-bly disputatious goal of teaching *for* internationalism nonetheless also seems realizable for the most part. How this goal can be realized in the existing circumstances of schooling is the mainstay of the final part of this chapter.

WHAT ARE THE OBSTACLES TO A DIRECT APPROACH?

As noted, it may be wise to avoid pushing too strongly for courses devoted solely to internationalism. Although worthy models of this focused approach have been successfully implemented (Long and King 1964; United Nations 1961), they do not appear to have reached more than a fraction of the num-ber of students enrolled in mainstay social studies courses such as U.S. His-tory (Thornton 2001b). Moreover, creating or adopting new courses can be difficult. For example, recently in North Carolina an attempt was made to consolidate two years of state history into one in order to make room for a new course on world cultures. Many saw this as a laudable attempt to use scarce time prudently while simultaneously assuring greater treatment of clearly useful international material. Critics charged, however, that it risked dangerous unfamiliarity with North Carolina's heritage by young people (Armstrong 2003, 135–136).

It is likely to be easier to utilize existing courses and curriculum than to innovate with new courses. The most common high school state mandates for social studies concern history, civics, and constitutions of the United States and the state in question. For example, Michigan state law requires that for high school graduation "regular courses of instruction shall be given in the constitution of the United States, in the constitution of Michigan, and in the history and present form of government of the United States, Michigan and its political subdivisions . . ." In addition, high schools "shall require a one-semester course of study of five periods a week in civics . . ." (Michigan State Department of Education 2003, 5–6).

Once we are set on utilizing existing offerings, the obstacles to sub-stantial instruction on internationalism do not, of course, vanish. The most obvious stumbling block to internationalism may be, as is apparent in the Michigan example above, the nationalistic and state (and sometimes sectional) slant traditionally associated with the American social studies curriculum. That is not to deny there is already material *potentially* relevant to educating for internationalism in the curriculum. But it is to say that this material has tended to be viewed through a nationalistic lens while minimizing internationalist perspectives. For example, in their treatment of foreign wars school history textbooks tend to stress and glorify the motivations and successes of the United States and ignore the motivations of other nations as well as minimize their successes (Billington 1966; Foster and Nicholls 2003; Harrison-Wong 2003; Walworth 1938). Sometimes these outcomes have been deliberate goals. At other times they seem the products of a variety of more or less uncoordinated, even unintended, forces.

When an American-centered curriculum to inculcate unreflective patriotism has been explicitly advocated, its corollary has often been censorship of other viewpoints (Rugg 1941). Both unreflective patriotism and censorship are undemocratic in intent and close off critical consideration of viewpoints other than those asserted by some individual or group as representing *the* American view. Unfortunately, there is a lengthy record of both in U.S. public education (Marsden 2001, 172–175).

Beyond avowedly political reasons, how schools work and the circumstances of teaching are significant stumbling blocks to major internationalist-directed curriculum changes (Thornton 2004). This is a huge topic and here I can only deal with three, overlapping aspects of it: 1) the importance of questions concerning what subject matter and activity may be significant for general education versus what subject matter and activity is currently favored by scholars in history or other traditional academic subjects; 2) a paucity of role models and good guidelines for desirable approaches to selection of subject matter; and 3) the myriad ways in which announced curricular priorities become lost in the daily grind of classrooms. Let me take each aspect in turn.

First, the purposes of the social studies in the schools are not identical to their cognate subjects in higher education. Nevertheless sometimes high school teachers refer to themselves as teachers of an academic subject such as history or another social study. For example, it is not uncommon to hear social studies teachers who mainly or exclusively teach history refer to themselves as "historians" whose job is to present as close a copy of college history courses as is possible at the high school level and, by apparent extension, claim historical significance as their basis for deciding what to teach. This is almost certainly an inaccurate characterization of what they are and the proper and actual scope of their professional responsibilities (Noddings 2003b).

Aside from deeply interested students who elect specialized study, history is in the curriculum to serve purposes of general education. Nothing in the subject of history directs us to which parts of it young people ought to study as part of their general education. Rather, we necessarily must look to educational criteria such as what history might be relevant to young people's individual growth, ability to get along with others, and understanding of current social conditions. Making good citizens and good neighbors is more or less the universally identified purpose of historical study at the secondary school level in the United States and is generally recognized as such even by historians who have become involved in curriculum design and policymaking for the schools (Watras 2004). Teaching history for college-appropriate goals rather than general education goals, however, persists in American high schools. In the almost certainly futile quest to bring all young people to "world-class" standards—defined as college preparatory work—many high school students are coerced into studying material in which they neither have an intrinsic interest nor see life relevance. The results of unhappiness, alienation, dropout rates, and so on are enormous (Pope 2001). Nevertheless, these failures seem to be taken by policymakers as signs that we need to buckle down still further rather than asking a critical question: Is there important material to study that young people might find relevant to their lives and the world in which they live? Failure to ask this question is probably not a hopeful sign for the alternatives to prevailing curricular emphases (Noddings 2003a; Oliver and Shaver 1966).

Let us examine just one manifestation of the disjunction between the aims we nominally profess and the curricular arrangements we actually provide. It is commonplace to justify the role of history and geography in general education because both offer opportunities to teach young people to think critically. At the classroom level, however, young people may encounter limited opportunities to engage with issues about which reasonable people disagree. A prerequisite of critical thinking is engaging with subject matter that is open-ended and somehow life-relevant: there must be a genuine question to be answered and some meaningful motive for doing so (Dewey 1991a).

In contrast, today's students are required to meet learning standards that prespecify what counts as legitimate subject matter. For example, they probably encounter the importance of Louis XIV or Prince Metternich in modern European political development. While, of course, this material *could* entail activities that involve critical thinking (and it almost certainly will for deeply interested students), activities designed to engage this kind of thinking are not always provided. Instead the material is often taught as closed, rather than open-ended, subject matter—that is, as a completed act of thought whereby the critical thinking has already been done by the textbook or teacher. The student's job, which many youngsters find unappealing, is to absorb the critical thought completed by someone else.

Meanwhile, all too often pressing global crises find no place in the social studies curriculum. For example, consider the ecological and human health catastrophe of the disappearance of the Aral Sea, which was once the fourth largest inland body of water in the world (Ellis and Turnley 1990; Kriner 2003). What has happened to this saltwater lake situated between Kazakstan and Uzbekistan over the past 40 years positively cries out for historical, geographical (both ecological and human), political, and economic investigation. How could humans have unleashed disaster on such a scale? What does the Aral Sea have to do with the Cold War, with nationalism? Can the shrinking of the surface of the Aral Sea be stopped, even reversed? Are there other "Aral Seas" looming? Of course, this kind of material is unlikely to appear in standard curriculum materials because it crosses the boundaries of traditional academic subjects and some communities might find it controversial. For all of these reasons, it probably won't appear on standardized tests.

Concerns such as these also raise a second obstacle to internationalism: social studies subject matter related to topics as complex as the Aral Sea require a sophisticated level of teacher content knowledge combined with familiarity with and integration of current events for which few teachers have been adequately prepared. Good guidelines for subject matter selection are scarce and, alarmingly, seldom a priority in teacher education even though knowledge of subject matter is, perhaps, the cornerstone of curricular-instructional competence (Thornton 1991). By "teacher education" here I am mainly concerned with the interconnection of subject matter and curricular-instructional gatekeeping, which includes the decisions teachers (and sometimes other decisionmakers) make about curriculum and instruction and the criteria they use to make those decisions.

Although the fact is rarely remarked upon in critiques of teacher education, most teacher preparation in higher education takes place in academic departments, not schools of education. Seldom do professors in academic subjects consider themselves teacher educators, however, let alone accept any responsibility for preparing their students for what the school curriculum contains. The models of what counts as worthwhile knowledge and legitimate methods of arriving at it modeled for prospective teachers will probably consist of the professor's critical distillation of his or her conception of the subject's proper concerns delivered by lecture. The tacit message conveyed for high school gatekeeping, it seems, is that knowledge is defined by others and the student's job is to absorb it. While this may work well enough for adult learners, it has long been shown to be ineffective with young learners (Barnes 1992; Wesley 1943).

Perhaps, of course, this gatekeeping model could be revised in light of what prospective teachers encounter in professional courses on teaching methods. Unfortunately this experience is likely to be confined to one or two courses. In any case, methods courses appear to have limited effects on how teachers think about subject matter and its arrangement. In a sense, however, this is scarcely surprising. To begin with, the academic courses teachers take outnumber methods courses by possibly more than 20 to 1. If time-on-task means anything, what teachers see modeled in academic courses vastly outweighs a meager encounter with alternative methods.

More broadly, in addition to taking undergraduate academic courses, teachers have likely been socialized from the early grades through high school to subject matter selection and arrangement that may be more familiar than it is effective for purposes of general education (Thornton 2001a). Even the best imaginable methods course, in these circumstances, would face almost insurmountable obstacles. But, in practice, methods courses are so overburdened with expectations of what ought to be accomplished and demands for quick fixes that they often become superficial hodgepodges that disappoint and frustrate instructors and new teachers alike.

A third obstacle to incorporating internationalism in general education comes from the expectations of policymakers, politicians, administrators, parents, college admission offices, and other stakeholders who push teachers in various ways toward conformity in curricular-instructional gatekeeping. Probably the most powerful pressure is, intentionally or not, for breadth of coverage. This is captured in the cliché about courses such as Western civilization or world history stretching "from Plato to NATO." The easiest way to satisfy social groups who claim to have been unjustly excluded from the social studies curriculum is to add a mention of them. Often coverage crowds out coherence and depth in subject matter, critical thinking, and connections of academic knowledge to broader life concerns. There isn't, many believe, time to do anything else.

Although there are various ways social studies teachers could respond to this pressure for coverage, most respond by speeding through a crowded curriculum in ways that often come across as superficial to students. Some teachers, however, buck the trend (Brophy 1993), and their experiences can be instructive for purposes of infusing internationalism in the standard curriculum. Specifically, this research suggests that with some imagination, a teacher can find numerous opportunities to treat internationalism in the high school social studies curriculum.

INCORPORATING INTERNATIONALISM INTO
THE CURRENT CURRICULUM

Although the high school social studies curriculum typically requires considerable work in citizenship, it customarily leaves topic and activity selection to teachers or other local gatekeepers. This is particularly the case with courses explicitly directed at citizenship such as Civics. Educators, academicians, policymakers, and other curriculum stakeholders frequently specify in detail what material should pass through the classroom curricular-instructional gate in the traditional academic subjects, especially history. Most educators who have thought about it at any length, however, recognize that citizenship education cannot be reduced to a fixed body of information. Effective citizenship education must be responsive to changes in society and adapted to local conditions. Its measure is taken not by knowledge acquisition alone, but by an assessment of attitudes and action (Dewey 1991b).

The most promising high school niche for infusing internationalism may be the existing courses. Examples of successful introductions of internationalism into such courses include participation in government or problems of democracy or Civics. Such courses are ordinarily designed for participation and inquiry, with topics properly varying because of changing times and particular interests of individual schools and classrooms. This kind of course constitutes a considerable challenge for the time, energy, and imagination of teachers who will usually welcome constructive suggestions.

As acknowledged in curriculum documents, many topics in civics courses have internationalist elements. For instance, New York specifies that its participation in government course should integrate "real and substantive issues at the local, state, national, and global levels" (New York State Education Department 1990s, 156). This language creates an opportunity to tackle global disasters such as the Aral Sea. Issues such as this provide a quick, discrete case study largely based on teacher-provided material. Alternatively, it could be an excellent chance for extended exploration in which students could divide up the topic and specialize in individual or group projects. One group might examine why the Soviet Union diverted the sea's feeder rivers and the connection to Cold War rivalry, another could look into the diffused responsibility for the problem since the end of the Soviet state, another might look to ecological change and any remaining ways to mitigate the extent of the environmental disaster, and so on. An interesting discussion could then ensue on what responsibilities we hold as stewards of the planet for environmental problems in other nations.

In courses such as U.S. History where the subject matter is more standardized, plenty of possibilities for adding an internationalist dimension still exist. One long-recognized method pairs a conventional topic in U.S. history with a current global problem (Gross 1958). For example, historic waves of immigration to the United States could be compared with the current issue of displaced persons and refugees. Similarly, the Articles of Confederation could be compared to the United Nations Charter or mining on the American Western frontier with the Bush administration's aspirations to drill for oil in vast tracts of the Alaskan Arctic wilderness where such activity has been forbidden.

United States history courses could also easily be amended in further ways without adding significantly to their length. During World War I, for instance, Herbert Hoover's wonderful humanitarian work feeding Belgians and other starving and displaced Europeans should be pointed to with pride as an example of American values admirably applied (Hofstadter 1967, 279–281). This brought Hoover, and the United States, universal admiration and prestige. (This example also serves to balance the oversimplified historical profile of Hoover as an ineffectual and hard-hearted president unable to face up to the magnitude of the Great Depression). In addition, during the same World War I period, emphasis could be given to President Woodrow Wilson's admirable, repeated attempts to secure peace among the European combatants, without any thought for national gain, prior to U.S. entry into the war.

AN EXTENDED EXAMPLE: NATIONAL SELF-DETERMINATION

In modern and contemporary history, it is difficult to imagine any topic that is more important than nationalism. It has, of course, a fundamental connection to civic knowledge and attitudes. In particular, over the last century or more, support for national self-determination has become axiomatic among members of the international community. There is no better place to examine national self-determination than the World War I era. This could occur in courses on world history, European history, and Western civilization as well as U.S. history. Without significantly diverging from subject matter that is routinely treated in standard courses, the theme of self-determination could add an engaging and important focus.

To illustrate how this might be done, let's consider one example in depth. The chain of events leading to the outbreak of World War I was, arguably, precipitated by national self-determination. In brief, some people from the recently independent nation of Serbia—and some of their fellow south Slavs who were subjects of the polyglot Austro-Hungarian Empire—were engaged in a struggle, by whatever means necessary, to secure national independence for the Slavic subjects of the Austro-Hungarian Empire. Even today few textbooks challenge the legitimacy of national self-determination per se in this context, even though this particular struggle led to a world war. Here at the outset of this instructional sequence, we can already raise a key question: What does "nationality" in the ethnic, religious, and linguistic cauldron of the Balkans properly mean, and who should decide? In other words, students should confront the dilemma that there were (and are) no self-evident national solutions that would be absolutely fair to everyone regarding the issues confronting conflicting parties in 1914 Europe.

The war underscored both nationalism and internationalism. Their interrelationship is nowhere more evident than in President Wilson's Fourteen Points, which he unilaterally proclaimed during hostilities to be the basic terms for a peace with the United States and its associated nations (Wilson

2003). United States social studies curricula ever since have usually concentrated on the 14th point, which addresses the formation of "a general association of nations." Even within this overarching internationalist principle, however, is another overarching principle: the sovereignty of member states in what would become the League of Nations.

As other points among the 14 make specific, the world community envisaged by Wilson, and many other idealists on both sides of the Atlantic, was nonetheless an internationalist community of sovereign nation-states. Indeed, the 14th point makes explicit that a "guarantee" of the security of each individual national state forms the core principle of the League. This fundamental principle was to have global ramifications.

An analysis of the 13th point, concerning the creation of a Polish state, best illustrates both the importance attached to and the problems inherent with national self-determination as a guiding principle. The third partition of Poland in the 1790s by Russia, Austria, and Prussia had ended Poland's existence as a sovereign nation. At the outbreak of World War I in 1914, Poles inhabited borderlands of the Russian, Austro-Hungarian, and German empires. In each empire, however, Poles constituted a minority group with inferior civic status. Clearly, the full intent of Wilson's document could not be realized under these circumstances because the boundaries between Germany and "Poland" were, from an ethnic standpoint, difficult to draw (Schapiro 1953, 744). Wilson's 13th point stated: "An independent Polish state should be erected which should include the territories inhabited by indisputably Polish populations, which should be assured a free and secure access to the sea." As map exercises would reveal to students, the obvious problem in fixing the border's location was that in many places the areas that were "indisputably Polish" were noncontiguous. There was no possibility of drawing a line on the map that had all Germans on one side and all Poles on the other. But this was only the beginning of the conundrum national self-determination presented in this case.

Even if a contiguous ethnic-linguistic dividing line had been possible, a land route for Polish "free and secure access to the sea" meant dividing Germany in two. The German region of East Prussia was severed from the rest of the nation by what became known as the Polish Corridor. It ran through an area that was justifiably Polish on ethnic grounds except that the only port then considered practicable—without which access to the sea would be meaningless—was the undeniably German city of Danzig (today the Polish city of Gdansk). In effect, application of the principle of national self-determination for Poland meant its denial for many Germans as well as loss of a contiguous national territory. Danzig became an international city administered by the League of Nations.

German resentment of these and other territorial readjustments with Poland was bitter. The bitterness persisted throughout the interwar years.

Indeed, Danzig and the Corridor were to be the immediate cause of World War II in 1939 (Taylor 1962) when Germany, quickly followed by the Soviet Union, invaded Poland and partitioned it for a fourth time. In 1941 Germany launched an invasion of the Soviet Union marked by brutality unparalleled in modern European history.

As the tide of battle turned against Germany, the Soviets were eager for revenge. By the end of 1944 the Soviet armed forces were poised to invade Germany. This invasion of eastern Germany in 1945 was especially brutal. Millions of the noncombatant population of eastern Germany were killed or injured by or fled the advancing Red army. This displacement was to prove permanent (Beevor 2002). What had been East Prussia was divided between Poland and the Soviet Union. Much more German territory to the west of the Polish Corridor was also occupied by Poland, which led to the ethnic cleansing of Germans on an unprecedented scale (Naimark 2001).

Presumably because Germany lost the war and was held accountable for war crimes on a vast and hideous scale, the school curriculum seldom deals with the massive changes in what had been eastern Germany. Instead the Nuremberg trials of war criminals and the rise of the Cold War are underscored. In these circumstances, perhaps it should not be surprising that American textbooks usually explain that Germany was divided into four zones of occupation. The fifth and sixth zones, land ethnically cleansed and settled by Poles and Russians, however, normally go unexplained (even though they are often marked on accompanying maps).

As the instructional sequence moves on to the Cold War, the suppression of national self-determination in Soviet-dominated Eastern and Central Europe continues almost to the end of Soviet domination in the 1990s. At that time, nationalism, which many had assumed effectively impotent, arose again. Its most visible effects have been, coming full circle, in the south Slavic lands of the Balkans where war and ethnic cleansing reappeared on a large and troubling scale. What this means for international peacekeeping and war crimes and the historical events related to them would be an appropriate current events topic to round out the unit.

CONCLUSION

While internationalism is, arguably, an indispensable element of any responsible program of civic education, new courses of instruction are difficult to establish. In this chapter I have argued that opportunities already exist for the substantial treatment of internationalism in the high school social studies curriculum. Utilizing these opportunities, however, seems to depend on provision of models from curriculum leaders and the exercise of educational imagination on the part of teachers. Therefore, it seems clear that what

responsible teacher educators need to do, including subject-matter professors who do not necessarily think of themselves as teacher educators, is focus on educating teachers on internationalism. Teachers should be acquainted
with a wide range of relevant curriculum materials, media, and instructional
methods as well as encouraged to regard questions of global civics and international events as vital across social studies topics and activities.

CHAPTER 6

A Letter to Secondary Teachers: Teaching About Religious Pluralism in the Public Schools

Robert J. Nash

DEAR TEACHERS:

What you will be reading in this chapter is my rationale for developing a graduate course entitled "Teaching About Religious Pluralism: Educating Religiously Literate, Global Citizens," which has become very popular at my university. I have decided to write this letter to you in a very personal and direct way, in lieu of a more formal book chapter. I know that many of you have wondered about how to derive some educational meaning from the calamitous events of September 11, 2001, both for yourselves and for your students. The terrorist attacks on the World Trade Center towers and the Pentagon, as well as the aborted terrorist assault on the White House, changed the geopolitical-religious landscape forever.

On a more microcosmic level, however, I believe that these events, as well as the continuing war on terrorism throughout the world, are also forcing us to reexamine the very core of what, and how, we teach middle and secondary students in order to help them become more globally aware, religiously literate citizens. What, you might be asking, does this type of citizen look like?

Let us imagine that this is a cosmopolitan person who is knowledgeable about, and receptive to, the complexity and richness of religious diversity throughout the world. This would be an informed and respectful person able to embrace what is good about religion and to disavow what is bad. This person is liberally educated and knows that it is impossible to understand the history, culture, or politics of most modern societies today if one is ignorant of the fundamental role that religion has played in every

93

country. Most importantly, this would have to be an ethically discerning person who realizes that much of what we in the United States believe to be moral—or immoral—is largely a legacy of the Judeo-Christian heritage, as well as of the European Enlightenment; similarly, what much of the rest of the world believes to be the crux of morality for themselves is based on the teachings of their own endemic religions and philosophies. Thus, our globally aware citizen is a person who is fully aware of the tensions in all religions throughout the world between what Nord calls "tradition and modernity, community and individualism, consensus and pluralism, faith and reason, and religion and secularity" (Nord 1995, 380). Above all, this is a person who is able to distinguish clearly between the corruption *inherent in* the very nature and structure of religion (e.g., inflexible and literal doctrines and readings of "sacred scriptures," identifying the "other" as enemy, and so-called "divine" claims of exclusivity on behalf of the possession of a final and absolute truth), and the corruption *imposed upon* religion by unscrupulous, extremist adherents.

As a growing reaction to that day when three airplanes became deadly missiles and a fourth was intended to be, we educators are reminded once again that we are, indeed, interconnected citizens of the world. No longer can any of us continue to think of religions outside the Judeo-Christian axis to be unimportant, or inferior, in the global scheme of things. No longer can we be content to ignore the need for religious and spiritual understandings in our school curricula. No longer can we, as teachers, afford merely to intellectualize religious and spiritual differences in a bemused or detached manner; or to adopt a folkloric approach with our students wherein we do some superficial ceremonial "sharing"; or to mention this content only in passing, if we bother to do so at all.

No longer is it enough for those of us who might be more cosmopolitan in our worldviews to do a whirlwind, textbookish tour through the three major monotheistic religions of the world in a world history course and let it go at that. In the global society we live in, we no longer have the luxury of thinking about religion as merely a private affair, something best left to the home, church, synagogue, or temple. And, finally, no longer can we marginalize the teaching of religions in our public schools.

At the beginning of the 21st century, the reality of religious pluralism hits each of us where we live. We must learn to deal with this new awareness with openness, respect, and critical understanding, or it could very well kill us. For Americans to be ignorant of militant Islamic fundamentalism, or of ultranationalistic Judaism, or of radical Hinduism, or of the proliferating extremist, evangelical-fundamentalist denominations of Christianity throughout the world, for example, is to court international disaster.

The events of 9/11 have thrown our provincial and isolationist American worldview, particularly its religious, political, and cultural elements, into turmoil. We have seen firsthand during the last few years what happens whenever starkly opposing religious-political conceptions of the world and human life collide. Whatever our previous views on world religions such as Islam might have been in the past, at the present time these religions signify something dramatically different and real for all of us. Whenever these religions remain true to their original, humane ideals, then they are a force for good in the world. But whenever they serve as engines for the escalation of cruelty and violence, they are an indisputable force for evil.[1]

RELIGION AS A POLITICAL FORCE FOR EVIL

Teaching about religious pluralism in an intellectually respectable way means that we need to be scrupulously honest about both the good deeds and the misdeeds committed in the name of a variety of religions throughout the world. For example, I have in front of me a handout of a very colorful graph. It depicts vividly the reality of religious difference throughout the modern world. In 1990, the World Development Forum asked the following question: "If our world were a village of 1,000 people, who would we be religiously, and in which continent would we live?" The answer is that we would be a village of 329 Christians, 174 Muslims, 131 Hindus, 61 Buddhists, 52 Animists, 3 Jews, members of 34 other religions, and 216 would claim no religious affiliation at all. Moreover, 564 of us would be Asians, 210 would be Europeans, 86 would be Africans, 80 would be South Americans, and 60 would be North Americans. Finally, as if to confirm the prediction that religious wars are inevitable in the third millennium, in this same village of 1,000 people, 60 would own one-half the income, 600 would live in a shantytown, 500 would be hungry at all times, and 700 would be totally illiterate (Eck 1993, 202. Originally cited in *Encyclopedia Britannica Book of the Year, 1990*). Revealingly, the vast majority of the "have-nots" would be the most religiously zealous as well as the most angry, while the "haves" would be content simply to assume a stance of benign, bourgeois neutrality toward religion.

On the global scene, whenever we mix fundamentalist and extremist forms of religion with politics, geography, economics, and the military, we get something volatile and lethal. Even a partial list of current-day religious-political conflicts is daunting in terms of the obvious threats to human life. To cite but two specific examples: the war against the imperialistic West waged by Wahabi Islamic extremists and the war waged against Al Qaeda and political terrorism by the United Nations and the United States continue unabated throughout the world. As the George W. Bush administration has said time and time again, the latter will be a war that could very well continue throughout the 21st century, reaching into all corners of the world. Direct military action began in Afghanistan in 2001. It threatens to continue throughout the infamous "axis of evil" countries, including Iran and North Korea.[2]

A second example of what happens when fundamentalist religion mixes with politics has been the continuing deadly strife occurring in India and Pakistan between Hindus and Muslims. The most recent wave of violence started in 2002 when a group of Hindu zealots, returning home by train to Gujarat from building a temple at the birthplace of Ram in Ayodhya, precipitated a fight with Muslim vendors on a station platform. The train was set on fire, and 58 Hindus died. In response, over the next several days, Hindus throughout western India killed more than 2,000 Muslims. With the ongoing struggle to regain control of Kashmir, the *contretemps* between Muslims and Hindus will probably continue to simmer for years to come. Hundreds of thousands of soldiers from both sides, for example, amassed on the Indian-Pakistani border in 2002. For a while, the world stood transfixed in fear of the prospect of nuclear war taking place between two of the most militarily powerful nations in the region. *The New York Times* proclaimed that if war had broken out, 12 million people would have died (Kimball 2002, 127).

Similar threats exist throughout the world. In Northern Ireland, Catholics and Protestants continue to injure and kill one another, sometimes in the name of politics and sometimes in the name of religion. In New Delhi, militant Hindus of the Save Dara Singh Committee often harass and kill Christians. On the island of Cyprus, Muslims and Orthodox Christians have been engaged in 35 years of armed standoff. In Armenia, Christians kill Shi'ite Muslim Azerbaijanis and Shi'ite Muslim Azerbaijanis kill Christians. In 1993, in Bosnia and in Kosovo, Serbian Christians engaged in organized mass rapes, summary executions, and ethnic cleansing of Muslim women and children All too often, Sikhs in India bomb Hindu aircraft, and Hindus open fire on Sikh temples.

One religious studies scholar has estimated that more wars have been waged and more people injured, killed, captured, or missing for religious reasons alone throughout the first and second millennia than for political, geographical, and military reasons (Kimball 2002, 156). Even if this is not completely accurate, a convincing case can be made for its partial truth. Whenever war reaches the point where it is waged as a holy cause, whatever the original reasons for going to war, then, even to objective observers, it might seem that religion and war are inextricably linked, and maybe even inevitably. This inference, of course, is a terrible mistake because at the heart of all religion is the promise of reconciliation and peace. Our students need to understand that whenever war throughout the world is conducted in the name of religion and declared "holy," whether by Christians, Muslims,

Hindus, or any other religion, then this is a good indication that the purity and goodness of each religion has been corrupted.

RELIGION AS A SPIRITUAL FORCE FOR GOOD

While this lineup of human atrocities committed in the name of religion is compelling enough reason for students in public schools to develop some basic literacy regarding the structural tensions within, as well as the differences between, many of the world's major and minor religions, it is not the whole story. Students also need to understand that religion and spirituality have the reconciling power to call forth that which is universally generous and decent in human beings everywhere. There is a common framework of positive values and ideals that bind all of the religions of the world together, even though this common ground is often difficult to locate amidst the competitive strife of so many exclusivist religious claims.

For example, most of the world's religions teach compassion toward the poverty-stricken, persecuted, enslaved, aged, and infirm. Most of the world's religions encourage charity and alms-giving to those less fortunate. The notions of social service and social justice have their origins in early forms of Judaism, Christianity, and, later, Islam. Moreover, all of the world's religions have engaged in some forms of moral uplift and humanistic social reform. Religions such as Christianity, Islam, Hinduism, and Buddhism have produced such world-transforming ideas as forgiveness, pacifism, peace, nonviolence, and compassion. Martin Luther King Jr. was an ordained Baptist Minister. Mahatma Gandhi was a Hindu and peace activist. Thich Nhat Hanh and the Dalai Lama are devout Buddhist monks and advocates of social justice who have put their lives on the line to advance the cause of peace in their respective countries, Vietnam and Tibet. Clearly, all religions have the potential to contribute to world peace.

Also, on a more spiritual, less institutional, level—and in spite of our cultural, religious, and political differences—all of the world's religions teach us that we are enmeshed in the same human experience together. We are all brothers and sisters. There is just no way out of the human condition with its incessant ups and downs, its struggles and disappointments, and its unending reminder that we need to discover deeper meaning and transcendent purpose if we are to weather life's storms. The world's religions have in common the understanding that we all share a similar drive to make and find meaning. We also have similar values, rooted in what secularists in the West call the principle of reciprocity, and what Judeo-Christian believers call the Golden Rule: Do unto others as we would have them do unto us.

The world's religions remind us that regardless of our social position or our wealth, we all hurt, and we all cry. During times of personal crisis and disillusionment, we live in the same dark cave of confusion and futility. Even when things are going well for us we sometimes fear the impending loss of our good fortune, the imminence of some unexpected catastrophe that will befall us and destroy our lives. Whether American, European, Asian, Middle Eastern, or African, all of us strive to locate the larger meaning that we hope actually exists in the midst of our broken dreams and unreachable aspirations.

For example, in the West, we are faced everywhere with a sterile hedonism and a competitive individualism that too frequently pits us against one another in the marketplace. This lonely state of affairs leads inevitably to a widespread numbness and despair, giving rise to runaway substance and alcohol abuse and record sales of prescription antidepressants and antianxiety, drugs. Also, faced with the grim prospect of deteriorating stock markets and a downward economy, corrupt multinational corporations, massive job cuts due to downsizing, an overreliance on foreign oil supplies, and a decaying natural environment, we experience very close to home the insidious worm that exists in the core of capitalism. It is important for our students to know that one of the major functions of all of the world's religions is to offer a more enduring, personal meaning to those who have experienced the spiritual poverty that often exists in the midst of affluence.

In less developed Third World countries populated mainly by people of color, there is grinding poverty and little hope for social justice and upward mobility. As we have seen over and over again in recent years, poor and oppressed people who live their lives in a constant state of hopelessness run the risk of being seduced by fundamentalist versions of all of the world's major religions and the assurances of salvation delivered by theocratic rulers.

In an existential sense, human beings everywhere seek consolation and comfort whenever we feel we suffer inexplicably, or whenever we feel that we stand alone in an indifferent universe. This quest for an enduring spirituality is endemic to the human condition. It is what sustains us, what inspires us, what gives us hope, what ultimately binds us together in a pluralistic world. Spirituality is the name that we give to the eternal quest for meaning that helps us to make sense of our finitude and our uncertainty. Spirituality is the breath of life that has the power to bring love to the world. It is the force that makes us truly human. For 3,000 years or more, human beings have experienced this animating force to love, create, and to believe in a number of venues, only one of which has been organized religion.

Our students must realize that religion, on both a national and a global scale, is always a mixed bag. It is capable of delivering so much that is beneficent and enduring, but yet so much that is maleficent and short-lived. Spiritual literacy begins with helping our students to understand that the cry for both proximate and ultimate meaning has been the one constant for human beings in all times and places. The words of Dorothy Allison are incisive: "There is a place where we are always alone with our own mortality, where we must simply have something greater than ourselves to hold onto. [We need] a reason to believe, a way to take the world by the throat and insist that there is more to this life than we have ever imagined" (Allison 1994, 181).

ADDRESSING RELIGIOUS PLURALISM IN THE SCHOOLS

Some of you might be wondering if the public schools are the proper place for considering the pluses and minuses of religious pluralism throughout the world. You probably think that the First Amendment of the U.S. Constitution requires a strict separation between church and state in America, thus ruling "out of order" any conversation about religion in secular, state-supported schools. I can only tell you that it does not. The constitutional wall of separation is actually a low, rather than a high, wall. While secular schools, like the state, must avoid favoring, as well as discriminating against, religion, they are free to study religion. I would argue that teachers have a right, indeed a professional responsibility, to help some understanding of religious differences find an educationally appropriate voice in schools. This, of course, should not be a voice that panders, promotes, proselytizes, or practices. Rather, it ought to be a voice that students can explore openly for its strengths as well as its weaknesses in the postmodern world, just as they do with any other kind of "voice" in the curriculum (Nash, Spring 2001, 1–20).

In the *Abington School District v. Shempp* Supreme Court decision in 1963 that outlawed school-sponsored prayer, Justice Thomas Clark declared that "Nothing we have said here indicates that such study . . . , when presented objectively as part of a secular program of education, may not be effected consistently with the First Amendment" (*Abington School District v. Schempp* 374 U.S. 203, 1963). This ruling suggests for all of us that we need constantly to try to achieve a salient balance between representing the pros and the cons of religions throughout the world. We should not favor one over the other. We need to create an educationally safe yet robust classroom space for what I will call "unbounded religious dialogue." This type of open, challenging, and respectful conversation begins with an acknowledgment that religion, for at least 3,000 years, has been a fundamental part of human existence. To exclude, minimize, deny, or trivialize in our secondary school curricula what has meant so much to so many human beings is to commit an act of gross educational malfeasance.

At this point, some of you may be asking yourselves a number of practical questions: Isn't this material too controversial, too value-loaded, for the public schools? Aren't we bound to offend a number of our constituencies, particularly parents? Why stir up the hornet's nest of fundamentalist special-interest groups in the community who will resist what they see as the encroachment of religious pluralism in the schools? Will administrators back us up, or will they sell us out at the first signs of trouble? Is it possible to teach about religion in such a way that we don't take sides? Also, what religions and spiritualities do we teach, and how do we do this? Won't we need special academic preparation? What if we ourselves are strong believers or nonbelievers? Isn't it inevitable that no matter how scrupulous we are, our own biases about this very provocative subject matter will get in the way? How can we get students to look critically at religions? Won't some believers, and even nonbelievers, feel disrespected? Do we public school educators have the same kind of academic freedom as our university counterparts to do this kind of teaching? Why not just avoid all these troublesome issues by putting religion on the back burner, and continue to maintain the noncontroversial, curricular status quo in the secondary schools of America?

Allow me to respond very personally to some of the questions that I raise above. And let me begin by saying that I have no particular answers that will satisfy all of you. I have been a professor of higher education for 35 years in a college of education. During this time, I have worked with thousands of pre-teachers, teachers-in-service, and administrators. Too many times in the past I have had to bite my tongue whenever religiously oriented questions have come up in my seminars. Whether it's in my philosophy of education course, my moral education course, my professional ethics course, or in my scholarly personal narrative writing course, sooner or later religious and spiritual questions arise.

Whenever I ask my students to consider what is truly important to them as educators—what pivotal values and principles they base their practices upon—religious and spiritual responses are unavoidable, if students are being honest. I push them to dig deeply even when they do not want to. I ask them what, in the end, gets them up every single morning and off to school, especially when their personal burdens are heavy and their professional work appears to be thankless.

This is the primary reason why I developed my religious pluralism course. I, an existential agnostic, wanted to come out of my own closet of religious denial and confront these questions openly with educators like yourselves. I wanted to enlarge my understanding of multiculturalism to include religious pluralism. I wanted to help teachers find a way to include the issue of religious pluralism in their work with students, along with such issues as racial, ethnic, gender, and sexual orientation differences. I wanted teachers to understand that if Americans choose to remain ignorant about what gives religious and spiritual meaning to people's lives throughout the world, then they open themselves up to the charge that they are completely out of touch with contemporary global realities.

I offer as anecdotal evidence that I have gathered from hundreds of public secondary school teachers these past few years the following facts: a large number of students in the secondary schools want to know much more about those religions that are different from the Judeo-Christian heritage within which most were raised. They want to understand what would drive some people to die, or to kill, for what they believe. They want to know why so much violence is committed in the name of religion; why so much hate is manifested under the guise of God's love; why religions can't seem to get along with one another instead of having to dominate all the rest. They want to explore alternative religions and spiritualities for themselves. They want a chance to find convincing spiritual answers to their worrisome existential questions about meaning, love, relationships, autonomy, careers, higher education, faith, peace, patriotism, and violence.

I sympathize with those of you who are asking the tough questions about the feasibility of taking on yet one more challenging responsibility in the classroom. It will be difficult, no doubt about it. Your fears are justified. I know from many decades of experience that when teachers first learned they were expected to teach other types of controversial subject matter—sex education, drug education, diversity education, citizenship education, environmental education, career education, political education—their fears were similar. Now such topics are *de rigueur* in most public school classrooms. I predict that, as painful as it might be at the outset, teaching about religious difference will become a standard practice in public school education. Our survival as a nation, with indisputably interdependent ties to other nations throughout the world, depends upon it.

I believe that the place for all of us to start in the schools is with a deeper understanding of the nature of pluralism. I think of *tolerance* as a minimal moral duty calling for a simple noninterference. It is the obligation to bear, or to put up with, different points of views and beliefs. I think of *diversity* as an empirical term that carries with it no moral obligation. It merely describes a state of difference or variety. It does not enjoin us even to respect this difference, let alone celebrate it, as so many educators think. *Pluralism*, however, is a thicker term than these two, containing significant moral meaning and implications for us as educators.

Pluralism, according to Diana Eck, aims to "build bridges of exchange and dialogue . . . and this must include constant communication—meeting, exchange, traffic, criticism, reflection, reparation, and renewal" (Eck 1993, 197). In my opinion, pluralistic dialogue about religions and spiritualities in the classroom, as in the world at large, requires direct give-and-take participation with all types of religious otherness. It insists that we allow the "other" to get under our skins, to engage with us, to disturb us, and even, if the circumstances warrant, to *change* us. Simple tolerance, respect, and celebration of difference must always give way to the active seeking of understanding, and a willingness to consider transforming or modifying our previous religious views. This approach to pluralism captures the spirit of unbounded religious dialogue that I mentioned earlier. Whenever conversation about religious pluralism with our students is too "polite," whenever it lacks spiritedness and candor, then something important is missing. We need to take one another seriously enough to ask the respectful yet hard questions about the things that truly give our lives meaning.

DIALOGUE IN THE CLASSROOM

I once witnessed a spirited discussion in a high school social studies class in my "Green Mountain" state on the subject of civil union legislation. Vermont is the first and only state in the country to guarantee same-sex couples all the legal rights and benefits of married couples. In a little less than an hour, everyone in this class of 20 students registered an opinion about the morality or immorality of same-sex marriages. Predictably, the more orthodox religious believers weighed in on the sinfulness of homosexuality and the biblically based sanctity of marriage between a man and a woman. And, predictably again, the secular skeptics scoffed at such "puritanism."

During this discussion, I deliberately counted more than 50 direct references to religion. A number of specific religious voices surfaced, including three Christian fundamentalists, a Reform Jew, an atheist, an agnostic, and a secular humanist, along with some mainline liberal Christians. Two gay students, recently out of the closet, also tried to make their views heard. It was obvious that all of these students had no practice in engaging in this type of dialogue, even though they were hungry to converse with one another. The teacher looked nervous, and in trying to be fair and neutral he at times lost complete control of the discussion.

The class interchange began with a simple ad hoc declaration of student opinions on the topic of civil unions. It then regressed to some snide name-calling and religious stereotyping. It managed to progress to a point where, with the teacher's well-intended encouragement, students tried to be polite toward one another. Unfortunately, however, the class hour ended in near-total confusion, much exasperation, and a few bruised feelings. It didn't have to.

It quickly became apparent to me that the vast majority of these students had no store of background religious knowledge they could call on in their respective analyses of same-sex marriages. Surprisingly, they knew nothing about their own religions of origin, information that might have shed more light than heat on the issue. In other words, they were religiously illiterate. In spite of this illiteracy, however, they still wanted to discuss the religious implications of the civil-union movement in their state. Concomitantly, I have also heard from scores of teachers that in many classrooms in our state, students are eager to learn more about Islam and its role in the Twin Towers destruction, suicide bombings in Israel, and worldwide proclamations of holy *jihad*. (*Jihad* is a much misunderstood term in the West. To most Muslims, *jihad* is a very personal term that denotes a spiritual and physical striving against evil. Rarely does it mean engaging in a religious war against others.) Many students in my own courses here at the university, to their credit, exhibit a healthy skepticism toward the far Christian right message that Islam is an intolerant, violent, even "vile" religion. It is for this reason that I have begun assigning the *Qur'an*, along with an excellent introduction to Islam, Akbar S. Ahmed's *Islam Today*, as required reading in several courses that I teach. I even heard one student in the above high school class ask her teacher why they hadn't read some Muslim literature for a current events assignment. No coherent response was forthcoming.

I know from my own experience here at my university that leading seminar conversations about provocative topics like religion—topics that are meant to be informative, invigorating, and respectful all at the same time— is a huge challenge for anyone. Add to this the embarrassing ignorance that plagues most Americans about religions in this country and around the world, and our overall educational task is daunting. Nevertheless, I believe that unbounded religious dialogue in the classrooms of this country is both desirable and doable, whatever its possible pitfalls.

Speaking from personal experience, it takes an obdurate will and a soaring enthusiasm, along with the courage to risk failure, to get this religious literacy project off the ground. It means understanding, and accepting, that you needn't be a religious studies scholar; you need only to be someone with a burning curiosity to read widely about religion and its enormous influence on the global condition. It means starting out small in the classroom. It means pushing the conventional curricular boundaries a bit.

Moreover, it requires asking evocative and challenging questions in the classroom in an authentic, open-ended way. It means building allies in your academic departments, as well as among administrators and parents. And, above all, it entails trusting students to learn how to be respectful of the content and of one another. This will happen in time providing that you, as teachers, are fastidious in presenting yourselves as model participants in respectful, critical, and open-ended religious dialogue.

All of this, I am convinced, is more than achievable, given the opportunity for you and your students to continually practice the art and craft of pluralistic dialogue in the classroom on *all* subjects, not just religious ones. I often ask my own students to watch carefully as we talk with one another in our seminar. What works and what doesn't? What will each one of them do to make it a better dialogue space for everyone, including myself? What do they think will work in their own classrooms when they go back home, and what won't? I also ask them to pretend that they will be asked by their school systems to construct a pedagogical primer for all the teachers in their districts on how to establish unbounded dialogue spaces in their classrooms for the purpose of facilitating religious and spiritual discussions. This centers their attention very quickly.

In the interest of truth in advertising, here is where I stand personally on the subject of religious pluralism. Whether we like it or not, in our democracy, opposing religious groups have a constitutional right to exist, as long as they don't harm others and themselves. Moreover, to paraphrase the well-known words of Thomas Jefferson, we shouldn't care whether our next-door neighbor believes in one god, 30 gods, or no gods, as long as he doesn't pick our pockets or break our legs. On the other hand, I believe that as teachers, we should be wary of those religious adherents who make unwavering, absolute truth claims, who demand blind obedience from believers, who claim to be in exclusive possession of "God's plan" for all of us, and who hold that their righteous end justifies any means to achieve it.

More to the point, however, I believe that there are just no definitive, empirical tests that can determine, once and for all, whether particular claims to religious truth are true or false, in the same way that there might be in some areas of science, for example. When all the absolute religious claims are made, and when all the efforts to convert others are exhausted, and when all the wars for religious supremacy have been fought to a bloody finish, the ultimate "truth" of any single religious view will always remain a profound mystery. In the end, as I pointed out in my book *Spirituality, Ethics, Religion, and Teaching: A Professor's Journey*, religious faith and belief can best be described as a metaphysical crapshoot, a blind, undemonstrable leap into the unknown (Nash 2002, 202–204).

One issue that we might raise with our students is the Hindu insight that although religious truth may indeed be one, there are an infinite number of ways to reach, interpret, and practice that truth. The oldest and most sacred Hindu text, *Rig Veda*, puts it this way: "*Ekam sat vipraha bahudha vadanti*," or "Truth is one, but the wise call it by many Names" (*Rig Veda* 1.64.46, cited in Eck 1993, 54). It would be fascinating to get our students' 21st-century take on this 3,500-year-old insight. I would bet that few high school students have ever heard of the *Rig Veda*. I know that very few of my graduate students have. It seems to me, however, that an open discussion of this pivotal Hindu axiom could help students voice their views on a number of religious topics, including religious relativism and religious absolutism.

In my own view, and in all my work with teachers, I assume that no single religion or spirituality has an exclusive claim on divine revelation or

Absolute Truth. To the extent that any religion helps its adherents to find the love, peace, morality, redemption, gratitude, faith, renewal, and compassion toward all others that we so desperately need to survive as a species, then, for me, that religion is a viable one for a global society. Of course, in a truly pluralistic classroom, even this assertion about what is worthwhile and viable about religion is open to debate. On matters of religion and spirituality, the only certainty I know is that I know nothing for certain. Thus, I ask my teachers always to put a question mark, or a vice versa, or ellipsis points, at the end of each and every one of my assertions, as I will theirs.

Finally, I promise my students that I will do my best to help them abide by the following ground rules for engaging in respectful, pluralistic dialogue:

- Every single person in my class, at least at the outset, deserves an obligatory, presumptive respect for any religious views expressed.
- We will display empathy and understanding at all times. Whenever we feel the need to push one another, we will proceed with the utmost caution always, checking in frequently with the person(s) we are challenging in order to inquire about their well-being.
- We will listen to one another intently, trying always to attribute the best, not the worst, motives.
- We will try to listen to one another critically and, whenever appropriate, to change or modify our own previous positions on religious and spiritual topics, given the intellectual and emotional force of what we hear. We will also learn how to tactfully change the subject whenever conversations grow too "hot" or reach a dead end.
- Ethically, we will commit ourselves to the principle that at all times we must refrain from going on the attack. We will proceed on the supposition that a genuine attempt to understand another's religious views must always be a prerequisite for critique and judgment of those views.

I close my letter to all of you with a very famous four-line verse by Edwin Markham from "The Man with the Hoe," written in 1899: "He drew a circle that shut me out—Heretic, rebel, a thing to flout. But Love and I had the wit to win: We drew a circle that took him in" (Markham 1899, 103).

I ask all my readers to consider the possibility that drawing a circle to take others in when conducting controversial conversations about religious and spiritual difference in the classroom might actually be the best way to reach mutual understanding and reconciliation. In fact, I challenge all of you to think of a better way than this to truly become global citizens in an interdependent world.

NOTES

1. See, for example, a study of Christianity's strengths and weaknesses from a historical perspective, B. Moynahan, *The Faith: A History of Christianity* (New York: Random House, Inc., 2002).

2. In his State of the Union address on January 29, 2002, President Bush identified North Korea, Iran, and Iraq as regimes that "constitute an axis of evil, arming to threaten the peace of the world." In the same speech, he went on to say, "These regimes pose a grave and growing danger."

CHAPTER 7

A Changing Vision of Education

Nancy Carlsson-Paige & Linda Lantieri

YOUNG PEOPLE ARE GROWING UP at a time when the environment, health, economy, nuclear weapons, and international conflicts are increasingly intertwined at a global level. What, then, is the role of schools in preparing young people to see themselves as part of this larger whole that includes not just their neighborhood, community, or country, but the world? Research shows that the nurturing of global consciousness requires that young people 1) experience a caring environment, 2) have opportunities to engage in decisionmaking and prosocial action, 3) see prosocial behavior modeled by adults, 4) develop skills such as perspective-taking and conflict resolution, and 5) have opportunities to confront injustice. Such knowledge and skills are constructed by children slowly and over time, beginning in their earliest experiences and evolving as children develop. These learnings are given meaning through the connections children themselves make. Yet today's educational climate of high-stakes testing means teachers spend more time teaching to tests, leaving less time for children to pursue such meaningful connections that lead to responsible global citizenship. Fortunately, the tools offered here such as class meetings; the infusion of critical thinking, problem-solving, and conflict resolution skills into academics; and the opportunity for children to take meaningful action in the world, as well as other promising curricular frameworks, can help schools teach academics in the broader context of serving the goals of global citizenship education.

In Quincy, Massachusetts, where many of the seeds of our nation's struggle for freedom were sown, middle school students at the Broad Meadow School banded together in a campaign to free Third World children from a life of indentured labor. It all began with the visit of a Pakistani boy named Iqbal Masih to their school. In a schoolwide assembly the young people sat in rapt attention as Iqbal recounted how he had been sold into bonded labor to a rug factory at the age of four because his parents were in debt. He told the children that his dream had been to go to school. Now, instead, at the age of 11, Iqbal considered himself lucky to be free to tell his story to others.

Two years later, fueled by the suspicious shooting death of Iqbal, these middle school students successfully mounted a campaign to raise both awareness and money to free other Pakistani children from a life of bonded labor. Using the Internet to gather support and donations from children and adults from around the country, the small group of middle school children met in the same church in Quincy where patriots had met to plan the American Revolution. As they held hands in a circle with the adults watching, the children shared their hopes and inspirations. They decided that with the substantial sum of money they had raised in Iqbal's memory, they would start a school in Pakistan for children who otherwise would never have an education. Because this group of young people decided to act, a school in Pakistan is permanently endowed, a loan program has been established for Pakistani mothers to buy back their children from bonded labor, and a United Nations resolution to toughen international child labor laws has been ratified by 132 nations.

This story may seem extraordinary, but we are living and educating our children in an extraordinary time in human history. Young people are growing up in an increasingly interdependent world. News from around the globe is available in an instant; the Internet and mass communications give young people instant access to ideas and people from all over the world. In addition, multinational corporations spread cultural messages to young people via this rapid form of mass technology. There is, therefore, an increasing awareness among students that a great many issues—the environment, health, the economy, nuclear weapons, international conflict—are intertwined at a global level.

The reality of our shrinking planet and its impact on young people has implications for how and what we teach them in school. We educators hold in our collective hands the responsibility to help young people become active, caring citizens of the 21st century who can understand that the future of their world depends on global cooperation and peace.

What does it take for young people to see themselves as part of a larger whole that includes not just their neighborhood, community, or country, but the world? How can we make schools places where children learn to make choices that support the individual and collective good and actively engage in making a meaningful difference? What is it that makes some children turn to such acts of conscience as the Broad Meadow School students did?

THE SEEDS OF GLOBAL CITIZENSHIP

In his book *Children's Social Consciousness and the Development of Social Responsibility*, Sheldon Berman (1997) talks about four basic processes that nurture and promote social responsibility and activism in young people:

- A nurturing and caring environment where children are involved in decision-making and prosocial action in the home and at school
- Modeling of prosocial and ethical behavior by the adults in a child's life
- Development of perspective-taking skills that allow young people to enter the world of another and identify with the victims of injustice
- Confrontations with injustice and development of effective ways of handling conflict

Schools are clearly one of the places where children learn what it means to be a member of a community and where skills such as effective ways of handling conflict, effective decision-making, and prosocial behaviors can be nurtured. But these skills and awareness are not lightning strikes or knowledge that one can pour into a child's brain like sand into a pail. Children develop an understanding of the social world through a long, slow process of construction. They use what they see in their lives as a basis for constructing an understanding of how people treat each other. New learnings continue to build on earlier ideas through a dynamic process in which increasingly sophisticated ways of dealing with social concepts and skills develop and gradually expand to include more of the wider world beyond children's immediate experience (Carlsson-Paige and Levin 1992).

The seeds for global citizenship are, therefore, planted early and nurtured throughout a child's life. As Berman points out, this kind of education "is not a list of values and behaviors we need to instill in young people, but rather they are behaviors and values we need to recognize and encourage as they emerge" (Berman 1997). Any discussion of how to nurture this sense of global citizenship must, therefore, look at how equipped schools are to play this sustaining role in the lives of young people.[1]

THE CHALLENGE

Our schools function against a backdrop of social ills that try the best of our intentions to teach for global citizenship. There is a widening gulf between rich and poor in the United States. For example, one out of five American children lives in poverty (Children's Defense Fund 2001). In such a society, stress of all kinds falls unevenly and unfairly onto children. A host of risk factors such as poverty, violence, racism, and poor health add up to what James Garbarino (1995) calls a "socially toxic environment" for many children. Law enforcement agencies in the United States made 2.4 million arrests of persons under the age of 18 in 2000 (Snyder 2002), and the Surgeon General issued a call to action in 1999 due to alarming rates of suicide in adolescents.

These risk factors are compounded by the negative effects of media culture with its aggressive marketing campaigns aimed at children and teens; corporations spend billions of dollars annually to market to this target group. Consequently, many young people growing up today, from the poorest to the most affluent, are imprisoned by our culture's obsession with material things. From an early age, they get the message that to feel good about themselves or to be loved, they need to look a certain way, to own the latest Star Wars toy or designer jeans. Young people have killed one another over leather jackets; children can be bullied or excluded in school for not wearing the "right" sneakers or t-shirts.

While schools may have been places in the past that helped young people cope with social risk factors in their lives, today's schools are increasingly driven by standards, tests, and accountability. Teachers spend more and more time teaching to tests; as the curriculum narrows, students have less and less of a role to play in their own learning. Instead of fostering meaningful discourse, exploring multiple perspectives, examining how power shapes worldviews, and getting to know ourselves and each other, schools today look more like what social psychologist Alfie Kohn calls "giant test prep centers" (Kohn 2001). In this climate, the aspects of the school curriculum that young people most need for the world they are living in and will inherit are disappearing: the social curriculum, multiple ways of knowing and being, multicultural curriculum, civic engagement, and global education. At the very time that young people need an education that equips them with awareness and skills to live in this global, multicultural world, the depth and breadth of school curriculum is shrinking. Fewer schools than ever now offer courses with a global perspective; in fact, many schools have cut back on social studies offerings altogether (Smith and Czarra 2003). At the very time that children and adolescents need support in dealing with the harsh world they are living in, a large number of educators are convinced that schools are failing them.

When the American Association of School Administrators asked 50 education leaders the following question: "What behaviors would students need in order to thrive during the next century?" civility and ethical behavior were among the most frequent responses (Uchida et al. 1996). In a similar international study of 267 global thinkers representing a range of cultural, religious, political, and spiritual perspectives, five shared values seen as critical to effective functioning in daily life emerged: compassion, honesty, fairness, responsibility, and respect (Loges and Kidder 1997). Thus, many educators do agree that the fundamental tasks of education go beyond academic achievement and keeping young people out of trouble. Yet we still have only a sketchy road map to show how values, civility, and ethics can be taught, or how to promote the knowledge, attitudes, and skills to bring about peace, nonviolence, and democracy in the world.

Despite these obstacles, there are educators who have been learning how to implement this kind of education for global citizenship. They are finding ways to teach the concepts, values, and skills of civic and global education as they provide each student with authentic experiences that actively engage head and heart. They are learning that schools can be places where young people practice constructive ways of being with others and learning about the world at the same time that they meet high academic standards (Aber, Brown, and Henrich 1999). Schools can be places that not only promote in young people a unity of one's sense of self but also an interconnectedness to others and a sense of meaning.

FRAMEWORKS FOR EDUCATING GLOBAL CITIZENS

How, then, do we begin to envision a framework for educating global citizens? One framework that addresses the set of concepts, skills, and behaviors young people need in order to nurture the protection of human dignity worldwide is the model provided by the Earth Charter, a declaration of fundamental principles for building a just, sustainable, and peaceful global society in the 21st century. The final version of the Charter was written through a process of worldwide dialogue. Meeting at the UNESCO Headquarters in Paris, the Earth Charter Commission approved a final version of the charter in March 2000. At a time when major changes in how we think and live are urgently needed, the Earth Charter challenges us to examine our values. It calls on us to search for common ground in the midst of our diversity and to embrace a new ethical vision that is shared by growing numbers of people in many nations and cultures throughout the world.

In terms of the concepts and content that need to be taught to young people across the globe, the Earth Charter lays out a strong foundation under the following four themes (Earth Council 2002):

1. Respect and Care for the Community of Life
2. Ecological Integrity
3. Social and Economic Justice
4. Democracy, Nonviolence, and Peace

The Global Campaign for Peace, launched at the Hague Appeal for Peace Conference in 1999, offers another useful framework that challenges us to make educating for peace an essential part of the curriculum. It gives us this charge:

A culture of peace will be achieved when citizens of the world understand global problems; have the skills to resolve conflicts constructively; know and live by international standards of human rights, gender and racial equality;

appreciate cultural diversity and respect the integrity of the Earth. Such learning cannot be achieved without intentional, sustained and systematic education for peace. (Hague Appeal for Peace 2001)

Imagine what might be possible if schools across the world took on such an "intentional, sustained and systematic education for peace." For the past 20 years, Educators for Social Responsibility (ESR) has been helping administrators, teachers, and parents carry out the charge outlined in documents such as the Earth Charter and Global Campaign for Peace in their homes, schools, and communities. ESR has developed a model called The Peaceable Classroom that highlights the skills and areas of focus needed to educate for peace, social justice, and global citizenship. The Peaceable Classroom is defined as a caring classroom community based on the following interdependent principles:

Building Community and Mutual Respect: Creating a safe and nurturing environment in which everyone participates and to which everyone belongs. Nurturing mutual respect among students and teachers becomes the starting point for creating a positive and effective learning environment and reducing adversarial relationships.

Shared Decision-making: Using a variety of decisionmaking processes in the classroom. Helping young people affected by decisions made to consider the consequences and implications of choices before making a responsible judgment.

Democratic Participation: Participating in nonadversarial dialogue and using controversy constructively. Encouraging open-mindedness and the right of everyone to be heard. Practicing the arts of compromise and consensus.

Social Responsibility: Acting on your concerns in ways that make a positive difference for oneself and others. Developing the convictions and skills to shape a more just and peaceful world.

Appreciation for Diversity: Exploring individual and cultural diversity in ways that help young people move from tolerance to genuine regard, appreciation, and acceptance of people who are different from themselves. Learning skills to become allies with others to counter bias, interrupt prejudice, and help build positive intergroup relations.

Affirmation and Acceptance: Finding ways to affirm the dignity and value of each person in the classroom. Helping students accept each other's strengths, needs, and idiosyncrasies.

Personal Connections: Creating ways to link personal stories, perspectives, and experiences to learning activities and outcomes. Developing personal relationships with each other and making time to stay connected.

Caring and Effective Communication: Encouraging active listening, assertiveness, and open, honest dialogue. Allowing time for students to disagree respectfully and hear other points of view.

Emotional Literacy: Allowing time for expressing and responding to feelings appropriately. Developing the capacity for empathy through perspective-taking and the inclusion of multiple points of view. Learning ways to manage emotions constructively.

Cooperation and Collaborative Problem-Solving: Using cooperative learning and collaborative problem-solving in ways that make each person's contribution integral to achieving the goals of the group.

Managing and Resolving Conflict: Helping young people to develop a "toolbox" of strategies and skills that help them manage and resolve conflicts positively, constructively, and nonviolently. Developing effective negotiation and mediation skills using win–win ways that meet the needs of all parties involved. Identifying options in a conflict situation.

In classrooms that promote the kind of education we are talking about, there is a congruity between content, teaching methods, and classroom structure. Each integrates and highlights the other. Young people develop the skills they need to problem-solve and then are given the opportunity and support they need to solve real problems (Lieber 1998).

A HOLISTIC PEDAGOGY FOR GLOBAL CITIZENSHIP AND DEVELOPMENT

The frameworks and principles described above begin to offer an outline for what global citizenship education looks like, but what pedagogical approach might best serve to implement the concepts, values, and skills described in these frameworks and principles? Guidance for implementation comes from cognitive researchers, the vast majority of whom subscribe to a constructivist view of education that emphasizes the active role of the learner in the learning process (Kohn 1999).

The mounting body of literature known as constructivist education is united by the central idea that students construct their own understanding as they actively engage in meaningful, relevant learning experiences; learners are not passive—they actively make their own meanings. Howard Gardner's theory of multiple intelligences expands our understanding of the multiple ways children learn (Gardner 1993). Not only do they read, write, and use numbers and logic, but children also learn through drawing, drama, music, social exchange, and inner exploration. Real learning is holistic, and real understanding emerges from active experiences that make sense to learners. Because of this, the developmental changes that occur over time in children and young people play an important role in the learning process. Knowing about development—how different age groups think and behave and how each student's development is embedded in family and culture—is a critical competency for global educators. We want the concepts, values, and skills of global education to be learned in a deep and genuine way that becomes part of each learner's repertoire for acting in the world. As David Elkind says, once growth by integration has been accomplished, it is difficult—if not impossible—to break it down (Elkind 1998).

The frameworks and principles discussed in the previous section encompass a broad sweep of concepts, skills, and values that cannot be taught directly from the outside in or taught quickly. These concepts, values, and skills grow over time; they look one way in a 5-year old, another in a 10-year old, and yet another in an adolescent. But they are built gradually in a hand-over-hand way, with new learnings building on earlier ones through a long, slow developmental process. David Elkind describes this growth process as a continuous one of differentiation and integration—separating out concepts and feelings and putting them back together again in a higher-ordered whole, a process, he says, that is time-consuming, conflictual, and laborious (Elkind 1998). And while all new learnings need to be practiced, the concepts, values, and skills of global education must be tried out, practiced, consolidated, modified, and refined every day. The essence of these learnings is in their application to real situations and in the connections to self and others that give them meaning. All young people have their own unique ways of seeing the world that are different from adult ways of seeing. Probably young children (preschool through 2nd grade) have a more radically different lens for understanding the world than any other age group. Jean Piaget helped us to see how unique the view of the world is before logic sets in (Piaget 1952). Young children can believe that the sun follows only them; they can believe they caused the thunder, or that they can put out a real fire with a pretend hose. This is because young children tend to think in a static way, one idea at a time; they have a hard time relating ideas in a logical way.

Piaget showed how young children think there are more pennies on the table if they are spread out and fewer if the same number is scrunched up because at this stage they make their judgments based on what they see and not on what lies beneath the surface (Piaget 1952). Thinking of one idea at a time makes it hard for young children to understand someone else's point of view—their heads are usually full of what they need and want. These prelogical ways of seeing the world have important implications for how teachers begin to bring the concepts, values, and skills of global education to their work with young children.

As children gradually grow into logical thinking, beginning usually around the age of six or seven, they begin to be able to think of more than one idea at a time, to relate ideas logically, and to understand causality and number; they now know that the number of pennies laid out on a table doesn't change when the position of the coins changes—they can hold onto the logic of the number despite its appearance. They can also think now about feelings and intentions that lie under the visible surface, can cooperate with others, and can follow rules; they can understand someone else's point of view, especially if it is in a concrete, immediate context.

Throughout the elementary school years, a child's ability to handle increasingly complex ideas grows slowly; children can think logically in relation to materials and activities that can be subjected to real activity. For a long time, children tend to reason about two properties or relations at the same time—they often look at problems as either/or propositions. So, although they have made many advances in thinking, they are still most at home dealing with concrete reality. Older elementary students love to examine problems of all kinds with data firsthand, to collect and categorize, to make detailed drawings of the world they know, to write and act out plays, and to learn about faraway places.

The gradual shift into more abstract thinking begins around the age of 11 or 12 and grows throughout the adolescent years. Thinking takes flight as adolescents begin to be able to think hypothetically and imagine possibilities they have never seen. They can begin to deal with abstract concepts such as democracy and justice separate from concrete experience. They can now imagine what might *be* instead of what *is*. They become interested in analyzing their own thoughts and motives, as well as those of others, and can use their new reasoning to examine several perspectives at once. They become more introspective and self-aware as their sense of self becomes more abstract: Who am I? What do I believe? What do others think of me? Am I accepted by my peers and the wider society? They open up to an expanded thinking that was not possible when they were younger.

These general developmental changes can guide educators in their work with students of all ages as children move very gradually from concrete to more abstract ways of thinking; from thinking of ideas one at a time to thinking about several ideas at once; from egocentric thinking to being able to understand the perspective of others. These changes develop in the context of each child's family and culture; they affect every aspect of a child's development—social, emotional, moral, and cognitive life. Coupled with principles of constructivist education, this broad developmental framework can guide educators as they approach teaching the core concepts, values, and skills of global citizenship education.

THE CLASSROOM AS A COMMUNITY

The creation of the classroom as a community of learners who work together interdependently in a climate of respect and creativity forms the basis of an environment where global citizenship education can be learned. Teachers and students live out the global ways of being, as described above in ESR's Peaceable Classroom model, in all aspects of classroom life. Teachers bring students into decision-making on many issues, showing how a "power with" model can work; students are celebrated for their cultural and racial identities and all perspectives are valued equally; social and emotional life is as important as cognitive ability, and space is made for integrating the head and the heart; and when conflicts and problems arise, a win–win approach is used to work them out.

In class meetings with young children, teachers play a very important role. They often pose problems for children to discuss such as this one: "There has been a lot of arguing and fighting in the block area lately. What do you think about this?" Because of their developmental level, children need help listening to one another's views, understanding how their actions affect one another, and finding solutions that the whole class feels okay about. But through the direct experience of class meeting and the teacher's help, children begin to lay the foundation for conflict resolution skills that will grow over many years' time (Carlsson-Paige & Levin, 1998; Levin, 2003).

In her curriculum guide entitled *Partners in Learning*, Carol Miller Lieber emphasizes how important class meetings are to the optimal functioning of a learning community in secondary school. High school students become able to take more responsibility for generating the agenda and facilitating class meetings. As they become comfortable, students can take on the roles of facilitator, summarizer, note-taker, timekeeper, and person who gives feedback. In so doing, they are practicing the many skills that have been used in class meetings throughout their school experience, but they are now integrating these concepts and skills at yet another level. High school students can hold meetings on many topics, some of which are unique to their age group such as discussions on hypothetical topics (e.g., "What would a world without wars be like?") and discussions about schoolwide issues such as policies, events, and ways to change the overall school climate (Lieber 2002).

The following example of a class meeting in a high school classroom shows students using the many skills they have learned from participating in class meetings to bring healing and resolution to a situation involving a classmate.

Raymond, a mediator from Central Park East High School in East Harlem, arrived at school one day profoundly upset and without his coat. He had left the subway stop near school and found himself surrounded by three guys who demanded he give up his jacket. The teacher called a class meeting immediately, with Raymond's permission, so he could share his story and express his rage.

Teacher: Raymond, I know you are very upset. Could you tell us what happened?

Raymond: I was getting off the subway stop right here in East Harlem and all of a sudden I was surrounded by three guys who told me that I better give them my sheepskin coat. One of the guys had his hand in his pocket and I thought maybe it could be a knife there. I don't know. (pause)

Teacher: Go on, Raymond. We're right here listening to you and all of us care a lot about you and what happened.

Raymond: Well, before I could even think, I started to unzip my coat, and I said to the guy who I thought had the knife, "This is incredible. I was just getting ready to do that"—you know, give him my coat. I said, "Who should I give it to?" One of the guys snatched the coat and all of them started to run off as fast as they could. Then, of course, I wanted to pick up some rocks and throw them at them, but I didn't.

Student: I can't believe you did that. I think you saved your life. How come you didn't try to say "no" or fight back? I think that's what I would have done.

Raymond: I don't know. It just came to me, but now I feel so angry and humiliated and I can't believe I don't have my coat. It's twenty degrees out there today and I walked three blocks without a coat.

Teacher: What do you think was happening for you, Raymond? How were you able to respond in this way and—I would agree with Marie—probably save your life? Remember, just last week this same thing happened in Queens and the young man didn't give up his coat and was shot to death.

Raymond: Well, I was actually thinking of what we were talking about last week of what makes violence even worse and that's more violence. I also remember you saying, "Remember, you are not your coat" last week when we were talking about what happened in Queens to that guy. So I guess I decided to do something that would deescalate the conflict and not give back more violence, and so that's what I did.

Student: Raymond, I think it was more courageous to not fight back and use your skills, but I don't know if I would have been able to do that either. And I feel angry, too, about your coat. No one has a right to take something that is yours. No one!

Teacher: So, Raymond, it looks as though you really put your skills to use in a horrible situation. And when you asked who you should be giving the jacket to you were also deescalating the conflict by staying neutral.

Student: How much was that jacket?

Raymond: Well, it was $119.

Another student: There are ninety-two seniors in this school—that is a little over a dollar each.

Teacher: What are you thinking here, Maria?

Maria: I'm thinking that if I had help I would be willing to collect this money for Raymond to buy another jacket. I think Raymond did the right thing, but how is he ever going to get another jacket?

Another student: I would be willing to help. I can't believe you were able to do what you did, Raymond.

Teacher: Well, this sounds like a wonderful plan. Do we need to do anything else to make it happen? How do you feel about that, Raymond?

Raymond: Wow. I can't believe you would all do that. But I know, given my mother's situation at home, I would never be able to buy another coat like this. Maybe don't ask everybody or say, "Only if you can afford the dollar." That would make me feel better, Maria.

Teacher: Sounds like a great plan. What are some things the rest of you are taking from this situation?

Student: These skills work, but you have to have them inside you, because you couldn't think that fast if you are in a dangerous situation like this. They have to be automatic.

Student: Also, it is better to get the anger out, just not where it is not safe.

These students are using many skills here—effective communication, understanding each other's perspectives, seeing problems as shared by the group, finding solutions that can work for everyone—that they can use and call on when they need them, skills they have developed over many years and that belong to them. The teacher's role is still very important, but it has changed from the class meetings of earlier years. The teacher here facilitates the meeting, setting a tone of compassion and trust. She asks open-ended questions that lead the students to reflect on their feelings and behavior with an abstract understanding they are now capable of using. The students share a deep sense of being in what Martin Luther King called a "beloved community," where they experience being their brothers' and sisters' keepers.

SOCIAL JUSTICE INSIDE AND OUTSIDE OF SCHOOL

Teachers can work with children of all ages on social justice issues both inside and outside of schools; as children grow and change, so will the approaches and techniques teachers use. An almost universal issue that arises
in the late elementary school years when children develop cliques and begin
to experiment with the dynamics of social power is bullying. Cruel, exclusionary acts against those perceived as different in some way will almost
always occur unless schools take active steps to counter this developmental
phenomenon. The "Don't Laugh At Me" program of the organization Operation Respect, founded by Peter Yarrow of *Peter, Paul, and Mary*, does
just this (Operation Respect, Inc. and Educators for Social Responsibility
2000). Through this program, children become sensitized to the hurtful
effects of ridicule, bullying, and intolerance that arise within their social
group. Through many different activities used over time—discussions, role-
plays, music, art, and writing—students come to look at the roles of bully,
victim, and bystander and to explore the feelings of each to reflect on their
own behavior and the behavior of others.

Social action can also extend beyond school walls to the wider world.
Rethinking Globalization (Bigelow and Peterson 2002) is a book packed with
examples of teaching about world justice issues to children as young as 9
and 10 years of age. In his fifth-grade class, Bob Peterson uses simple stories
and a problem-posing approach to help students connect their own lives to
the lives of children they don't know. He tells his class that 30,000 children
die daily from malnutrition and preventable illness. He asks, "How many
schools with the same student population as ours would it take to equal the
number of children who die each day?" In this way he creates a math lesson
just right for his students' developmental level that helps raise their awareness of social justice in a way that fits with their development.

To begin to introduce issues of globalization, a complex topic that many
would say is too abstract for fifth graders, Bob Peterson places a shopping
bag in front of the class and asks the students to guess what's inside. Out come
a t-shirt, a McDonald's Happy Meal toy, and a Nike shoe. He asks how far
these items have traveled. At first students answer, "from McDonalds" or
"from the store." Then he has students come up and read where each item is
from. As a class they locate the country on the world map. For homework,
students do a "Where Are My Things From?" activity in which they list 10
household items, the brand names, and where they are made. In school,
they share their lists and label and color maps that show the origins of their
things. These activities integrate developmentally appropriate math, reading, social studies, and science skills. Later, he shows the video *When
Children Do the Work* (1996), which portrays the harsh conditions child

workers endure. He uses photos of child laborers to spark poetry writing. These concrete experiences connect these fifth graders to other children in the world and a larger social justice issue. Invariably the students ask, "What can we do?" and he helps them figure out how they can write letters, buy things made in places that don't use sweatshops, educate young children about the issue, and set up their own organizations. One year his students set up the "No Child Labor Club," which included third, fourth, and fifth graders. Among other things, they marched at a rally sponsored by labor organizations against NAFTA, and two of the children spoke there.

Bill Bigelow of Rethinking Schools is a brilliant curriculum developer and high school teacher who has designed many different activities for his students on globalization, which are presented in *Rethinking Globalization*. With the help of these activities, secondary students begin to discover some of the abstract economic and political concepts underlying globalization. Through participation in a simulation that he invented called *Transnational Capital Auction: A Game of Survival*, Bigelow's students learn how governments lure transnational corporations with attractive investment climates that maintain low wages, use child labor, and harm the environment. Through acting out roles as Third World elites trying to attract corporate investors, students come to understand abstract concepts such as capital and the complex social, economic, and ecological consequences of globalization. They look at global sweatshops and, through poems and videos, see the lives behind the products they buy. Students are encouraged to write in the voices of those who make these products for pennies an hour—clothes, soccer balls, and Barbie dolls—and to feel what their lives are like. Students look at the "Nike Code of Conduct" and do a "loophole search" that makes full use of their critical thinking skills. Toward the end of the unit, Bill steers his students to their final project—to do something positive with the knowledge they have gained. He gives them a "Making a Difference" assignment sheet full of possible ways to take action within or outside of school.

Some of the projects students have developed include giving presentations on global issues to other classes, writing articles for local papers, and writing letters to Phil Knight, CEO of Nike, and to Disney. One student discovered that at the five nearby Portland schools, the soccer balls were made in Pakistan, where children as young as six work in factories making these balls. Some children working in the factories are sold and resold as virtual slaves and treated with extreme cruelty. This student wrote to the school district's athletic director describing the conditions under which the soccer balls are made and asked school officials to rethink their purchasing policies.

This entire unit captures the developmental energies of adolescents: their sense of justice and their ability to imagine a better world; their ability to think abstractly and critically and to relate several complex ideas together; their ability to empathize with how someone else feels and to imagine their life through role-plays, drama, and writing. This unit captures the momentum unleashed by the developmental changes of adolescence and gives it meaning and purpose through new knowledge, awakened compassion, and social action.

A VISION OF A POSITIVE FUTURE

The good news is that inspiring educators such as Bob Peterson and Bill Bigelow are showing us how to put the principles of global peace education into practice with real curriculum content for students of various grade levels. They show us how schools can teach academics in a broader context of social values. They inspire educators to pursue a kind of teaching that will outlast test scores. But we need to work in order for these exceptions to become the norm in education today. We need to insist that schools develop policies and approaches that enable all young people to have their ethical, political, social, and emotional selves welcomed, their spirits uplifted, and their capacity for active, meaningful learning fully engaged as a normal, natural part of their education. We need nothing less than compassionate, insightful, and committed young people and adults who will learn how to do the extraordinary things necessary to tackle the profound political, emotional, social, and spiritual issues of our time. Our task as educators who are preparing young people to be global citizens is to make sure that no child is left behind and that every aspect of the human being is welcomed into our schools.

As 1999 drew to a close, the final meeting of the UN General Assembly declared the first decade of the new millennium the "Decade of the Culture of Peace and Nonviolence for the Children of the World." With this challenge, our work is clearly cut out for us. Our task is to figure out what actions we can take today in our own sphere of influence to educate our children to think, act, and feel first as global citizens and second as national citizens. Becoming a citizen of the world involves a change in consciousness. As Parker Palmer often says, we are "living in an ecosystem much larger than a neighborhood or nation." We are all one. Our best hope for humanity is to fully engage young people with this global reality in ways that interest and inspire them to understand themselves, others, and the interdependent world in which they live; to come to love and believe in justice and peace; and to take active steps in their own lives to bring about a better world.

NOTE

1. See "A Holistic Pedagogy for Global Citizenship and Development" below for further discussion.

What Have We Learned?

Nel Noddings

I WILL NOT ATTEMPT a full summary of the individual chapters because each author has already done that job. However, it is useful to revisit some promising recommendations and ask about their possible implementation in today's schools. After that, I want to extend the discussion of obstacles to educating for global citizenship and make a few final suggestions.

THE RECOMMENDATIONS

Possibly the most important recommendation, made by every writer in some form, is to recognize the power of the local in building a global perspective. When students learn to respect and befriend classmates from different backgrounds and cultures, they are learning an attitude significant for global citizenship. When they learn to study and care for their own backyards and neighborhoods, they are preparing to study global ecology. Again, mastering the techniques of conflict resolution in classrooms should inform later approaches to world conflict.

The local can inform the global. But the reverse is also true. Sometimes it makes pedagogical sense to start discussion with events at some distance and then move to the local. Students studying the tragedy of the Aral Sea (see chapter 5 and Ward 2002), for example, may be sufficiently alarmed by the devastation of that once great body of water to question practices involving water use in their own regions. Similarly, debates about religious practices might be eased by starting with distant or little-known religions. Are there beliefs we quickly dismiss as ridiculous? Do we hold beliefs that others find ridiculous? How credible are their criticisms?

Although several of us have mentioned John Dewey and, perhaps, even identify ourselves as Deweyans, our recommendations do not insist on starting with the local and moving outward. Rather, we suggest analyzing each theme and concept to find the best place to begin. Dewey was right, I think, in insisting that our teaching must take account of what students already know, are interested in, and are able to do. But he does not give enough attention to their imaginations. A wonderful story set in a foreign time and place—even in an imaginary place—may be the perfect beginning for some explorations. If the stories are wisely chosen, they can also add to historical knowledge that might be deferred indefinitely under a rigid local-to-global regime. This is at least part of Kieran Egan's (1999, 2003) criticism of the expanding horizons curriculum for social studies. Dewey would almost certainly welcome our continuing analysis, critique, and revision of earlier ideas on curriculum and methods.

Another suggestion that appears in several of the preceding chapters is that material on global citizenship be incorporated into existing courses. Several of us made this point explicitly. (See, especially, chapters 2 and 5.) The reason for this is not that new and specialized courses are not desirable but, rather, that the crowded condition of the school curriculum makes it likely that such additions would be (reluctantly) rejected. It is this difficulty that causes so many promising elementary school topics to disappear at the high school level.

But is not the same problem replicated at the level of existing courses? Isn't it almost as hard to add material to the cluttered courses we already have as it is to add new ones? In reality, it is. But it shouldn't be. No course should be rigidly constructed and impervious to timely revision. Moreover, it is a mistake to restrict teachers to a curriculum that is entirely prespecified. Good teachers need the flexibility to introduce new material and discard old in accordance with the needs of their students and shifting events.

Curriculum integration need not be restricted to single courses. The temptation is to suppose, for example, that the social studies curriculum must bear full responsibility for citizenship education. But a careful analysis of relevant topics suggests that the burden (and rewards) should be shared across the curriculum. Certainly, science has much to say about ecological concerns and, properly handled, it could contribute to a healthy discussion of science and religion; it should also be expanded to include psychology. Classes in literature can include novels, essays, and poetry that describe the love of place and its significance in human flourishing. Literature is also a medium without peer in the treatment of existential and moral questions. Even mathematics—the most closely defined of all subjects—can include a study of birthrates, incomes, comparative health data, war casualties, the cost of social programs, systems of taxation, and appropriate means for collecting and evaluating such data. It is, perhaps, obvious that foreign languages, art, music, and sports can be used to enhance global understanding and appreciation. What is needed is a school-wide commitment to include such material in the curriculum.

Curriculum analysis should include not only a careful study of topics and themes but also the skills and attitudes likely to enhance a global perspective. The open, problem-solving approach recommended earlier seems fundamental for global citizenship. However, a commitment to this approach has benefits far beyond more generous citizenship. It is useful in maintaining a healthy marriage, parenting, friendship, and professional life, and its generalizability should be pointed out at every opportunity. It is almost always better to ask, What is the problem and how can we solve it? than to seek out and blame the guilty or dwell on the mistakes of others. Thus, educators can contribute to global citizenship even when the topic at hand is something very different, and it is part of our responsibility as educational theorists to consider the generalizability or transferability of the skills and attitudes we seek to develop. (It should be noted that when I speak of transferability, I am referring to *potential* transfer; there is no guarantee that a particular skill will actually be transferred to a new domain.)

Other skills that should be generalizable include listening, couching criticism in constructive terms, and extending sympathy to those in pain. Not long ago, I heard a father severely scold his little boy for riding his bicycle into a sand drift on the boardwalk. The child fell, of course, and got a scraped knee, but the father expressed no sympathy for the hurt. Instead, he shouted coldly, "Didn't I tell you to watch for these sand patches?" It would have been far better for their relationship if the father had kissed the hurt knee and said, "We've gotta watch these spots." Similarly, on the world scene, perhaps we spend too much time fixing blame and refusing sympathy to those who, in our opinion, are getting their just deserts.

Criticism can be given both sympathetically and constructively. Too often criticism is either destructive or withheld entirely. I'll say more about the latter in the discussions to follow on gender, war, and religion. The skill of giving constructive criticism is best learned from the example set by parents and teachers, but children need lots of practice in developing their own skills at criticism. Formal opportunities to respond to peers should be provided in most courses, and the responses should be preceded by explicit instructions: first, listen carefully so that you are sure of what has been said; ask for clarification if needed; identify strong points; make suggestions that might make the presentation even stronger. If you locate an error, point it out gently: I think that date may be wrong, or, I think that poem is by Frost, not Sandburg, or, let's check these figures again. Above all, if we want students to develop the skills of constructive criticism, we have to model the skills. The result should be eager students who are unafraid to express themselves in public.

The question arises as to whether and how we can use these important skills in discussing topics central to global citizenship. The preceding chapters all give considerable help on this, but I want now to extend the discussion by revisiting some of the topics that present the greatest obstacles to educating for global citizenship.

GENDER AND MORAL COMMITMENT

Should a Muslim woman be forced to remove her veil for a driver's license photograph? Recently, such a case arose in Florida, and the eventual outcome is unclear. A photograph that shows only a person's eyes is very nearly useless for identification purposes. But forcing the removal of a veil may be regarded as a sign of disrespect to the candidate's religion. Possibly most of us would agree that the veil must be removed. After all, the woman is free to refuse, but if she wishes to obtain a driver's license, she must agree to the requirements. But are "most of us" right in this decision? How should we defend it?

In the next section, I will return to issues of religion in connection with global citizenship. Here it may be enough to point out that questions of gender, religion, and national origin are not easy to separate. In liberal democracies, there is a growing commitment to the equality of men and women, and although much still needs to be done, a majority of our citizens express at least verbal assent to the commitment. Those who openly disagree usually refer to religious precepts to support their position. Should public schools advocate openly for gender equality?

If this issue is discussed (and I think it should be), students will need to be reminded that moral relativism is not a logically viable option. As we pointed out earlier, almost none of us would be comfortable shrugging off cannibalism, gruesome torture, slavery, honor killings, or child abuse as "just their way"—a cultural difference to be tolerated. Further, careful study should convince students that human beings have made some moral progress over the centuries. We no longer hang young children for thievery, exhibit the heads of executed prisoners on pikes, confine the mentally ill to filthy cages, disembowel condemned prisoners, enslave subordinate populations, forbid women to own property, or insist that there is no such thing as marital rape. It could be argued that some of these changes are motivated more by aesthetic than moral sensitivity. We just don't have the stomach for flaying people alive, burning them, or disemboweling them. If our decisions were motivated by moral conviction, then we wouldn't do these things at a distance by dropping bombs or planting land mines. Still, the progress is not all and simply aesthetic, and there is no reason to denigrate the aesthetic if it enhances our moral sensibility.

Is it right, then, to regard the equality of men and women as a moral imperative—something we should advocate and work toward globally?

Certainly this seems correct in a liberal democracy, and public schools as instruments of the state must promote such equality. What should we do, then, when some parents disagree?

In *Starting at Home* (Noddings 2002), I discussed the case of *Mozert v. Hawkins*, in which a group of Christian fundamentalist parents brought suit against a school board for allegedly undermining their free exercise of religion by requiring a reading text that included material contrary to their religious beliefs. The parents had several complaints, but one is especially interesting here. They objected to "gender role reversal" in the text. For example, the illustration for one story showed a boy cooking while his sister read to him. The parents volunteered to come to the school and, using an older text, supervise reading sessions for their own children. Should they have been allowed to do this?

The courts ultimately decided against the parents, primarily on the grounds that allowing such an exception would lead to many more and, thus, to chaos in school management. If we set aside the legal issues momentarily, what moral position should we take?

On the one hand, as citizens of a liberal democracy, we are committed to the free exercise of religion. On the other, we are also committed to gender equality. Can we permit girls to be schooled in such a way that they never gain the critical thinking skills needed to make an autonomous decision about their roles in society? Because private schooling is allowed for those families who can afford it, there is little we can do to protect girls from sex-role discrimination in nonpublic schools. But surely public schools should not permit this.

In *Starting at Home*, I took the position we have been advocating here: Without denying our moral commitment to gender equality, we should try to keep the lines of communication open. Without coercing, we should keep trying to persuade. This is what I suggested:

> Suppose the school principal has a real dialogue with the worried mother, call her Ms. B. The principal listens. She disagrees with Ms. B, but she acknowledges the genuineness and depth of her convictions. She says, in effect, "Okay. We'll allow you and other mothers to come in and teach your children reading from the older text. But you have to understand that these situations will arise again and again. We *do* believe in equality for women, and that belief is bound to emerge in other contexts. However, we want your children to remain with us, so let's try your plan and see how it goes." (Noddings 2002, 77)

In contrast with the court-ordered decision—one that tore apart a community and resulted in the withdrawal of some students from the public school—my solution advocates "staying with," maintaining friendly relationships across disagreement, and at the same time asserting and reasserting our commitment to gender equality.

The same approach might be applied globally. We should not simply shrug off gender inequality anywhere as "just their way" or as justified by religious beliefs. Students should be reminded that even in this country—and not long ago—women were legally denied equal rights on religious grounds. But neither should we impose our views by political force. Conversation, patience, friendship, and education provide avenues to progress.

RELIGION

The need for religious tolerance is obvious—at least, it is obvious in a liberal democracy. In the United States, freedom to practice a religion or to reject religion entirely is guaranteed by the Constitution. It is hard to imagine how global citizenship might be encouraged from a perspective that denies this right. Yet theocracies and threats of theocracy continue to appear in the 21st-century world.

The continued presence—even growth—of theocratic thinking suggests a need for understanding, but perhaps not tolerance. As several of us have pointed out, moral relativism is not a viable position, and if we believe that people should be free to choose their own positions on religion, we have to promote religious freedom. Again, promotion or advocacy does not require coercion, ridicule, or indoctrination. It requires continuous efforts at friendly and powerful education.

The connection between religion and gender should be studied carefully, and this can be done through biographies, essays, and histories. Sattareh Farman Farmaian, writing of her girlhood in Iran, describes her anger and humiliation when her father rejected her request for further education (she was an outstanding student), saying, "It would be a waste of money . . . She is a woman. A woman will be nothing" (Farman Farmaian 1992, 90). Hearing such a statement, students may react with disgust and contempt toward Islam. It is hard to develop a sensitivity for ambiguities that will promote critical appreciation for the beliefs of others. We need to hear more than this cruel statement about women.

It is unusual, however, for people to develop critical appreciation for even their own religions. Many people grow up believing that any form of criticism is a sign of heresy or incipient apostasy. For perhaps the majority of adults, the two words *critical* and *appreciation* are at odds; they cannot be reasonably joined.

Teachers should not *preach* critical appreciation. Rather, they should help students to recognize the possibilities by reading and hearing powerful voices that exemplify critical appreciation. Studying other religions sometimes triggers reflection on one's own:

President Andrew Dickson White of Cornell recalled that his belief in Christ's miracles, on which Christian truth seemed to depend, collapsed in the 1850s when he learned that Islam claimed the same sort of evidence for its doctrines. (Turner 1985, 155)

Does such recognition destroy faith? Sometimes. But students should be made aware that the analysis of miracles and myths can also deepen faith. Among the many contributions of literature studies, the discussion of myths surely stands in the first rank. The great myths should not be presented as either falsehoods (believed by "other" people) or stories concocted to explain natural phenomena not yet understood. Rather, myths—separated from historical accounts—acquire essential meanings and help us to understand the human psyche and condition (Jung 1969; Ricoeur 1969). Great themes that appear again and again include fear of the king or father, sacrifice of the son, creation, immortality, magic and witchcraft, ritual eating of the god, the sacred marriage, and embodiment of evils and their expulsion (Frazer 1951).

Students in the United States are sometimes upset when teachers refer to the myth of Adam and Eve. "That's not a myth!" some will protest. They must be helped to understand that the label "myth" is not an insult but, instead, an acknowledgment of universal interest in the origins of life. Teachers interested in the connections between religion and mythology can find many books to help them (Noddings 1993). For present purposes, we should emphasize that an appreciation of the role of myth in religion (including one's own religion) may contribute substantially to the attitudes required for global citizenship.

Before closing this section, I want to return briefly to the discussion of gender and religion. If students are shocked by the statement of a Muslim father on his bright daughter's future, they should be reminded that all of the world's great religions have discriminated to some degree against women. I can remember how I (in my 40s) reacted to Mary Daly's *Beyond God the Father* (1974) with both shock and appreciation. Why had I not heard these things before? Why had they never appeared in my earlier education?

This topic, religion, is perhaps the most difficult of all subjects for teachers to approach. Robert Nash has shown in chapter 6 that it is possible to discuss religion with college students. I think it is also possible—even necessary—to do so with high school students, but I do not underestimate the difficulties we face.

WAR AND VIOLENCE

American students read and hear a lot about wars. Indeed, the history curriculum is sometimes described in war-referenced chronological terms—

for example, from the Revolution to the Civil War. When conflict is treated as a controversial issue, students are invited to consider several points of view fairly. In recommending that the Vietnam War be presented as a controversial issue, Thomas Lickona endorses the approach of the Center for Social Studies Education: "Learn the facts about the controversial issues involved in the war. Consider all points of view and identify the assumptions behind the different viewpoints and the values behind the assumptions. Research the backgrounds of the persons who held the different views of the war" (Lickona 1991, 270). This could provide an exercise in critical thinking except for the fact that the Vietnam War is not a critical issue for most of today's high school students. For them, it is ancient history, and the discussion recommended has limited usefulness. It is not what students need most.

What young people need to consider are matters relevant to their own lives—such matters as the meaning of patriotism, an understanding of propaganda, the psychology of war and the way it dulls or destroys moral responses, and compassion for the enemy. If these matters can be addressed in a unit on the Vietnam War, the study may come alive for students and contribute to their growth as global citizens.

What does it mean to be patriotic? Does patriotism consist of flying the flag, reciting the pledge of allegiance, and claiming that one is "proud to be an American"? Teachers need not dismiss these familiar signs of patriotism as irrelevant, but they must help students to understand that genuine patriotism may take very different forms. In chapter 1, Peggy McIntosh points out that the "for us or against us" attitude of the Bush administration on the Iraq war is not conducive to global understanding. Many thoughtful people who love their country have opposed its wars and objected strenuously to the erosion of liberties that often accompanies war.

The discussion should be motivated by current events, but it would be helpful if teachers were aware of historical examples of dissent and repression. Because most teachers are at least acquainted with the work of John Dewey, it would be useful to review and to share with students the story of dissent at Columbia University during World War I. Professors James Cattell and Henry Wadsworth Longfellow Dana lost their jobs for disagreeing with President Butler's wholehearted advocacy of the war. The eminent historian Charles Beard resigned in protest. Dewey, while deploring Butler's high-handed methods, tried to steer a middle course (Westbrook 1991). Which of these men should be regarded as a patriot?

I include references to events during World War I because I want it to be clear that although curriculum topics should be genuinely controversial in present life, it can be powerful pedagogically to move from contemporary to historical events and vice versa. There are many important lessons to be learned from the study of political repression during past wars, and without these lessons students may be unable to assess current events such as the recent Patriot Act and the castigation of writers who spoke up forcefully against the invasion of Iraq.

Every citizen should acquire an understanding of propaganda and its power to influence opinion. Not incidentally, such understanding can be extended to a study of advertising and its effects on consumer behavior. Do we really need the arsenal of drugs regularly advertised on television, or are we becoming a nation of drug-dependent followers? Why do so many of us drive SUVs even though we suspect that they are dangerous and know that they use too much gasoline? Why do poor kids spend their hard-earned money on expensive brand-name clothing when they could dress well for far less? Addressing these questions should help to develop the habits of mind required for critical thinking, and, of course, they are important in themselves.

Although it is troubling to look at old war posters and to listen to war slogans, it is important that these be part of education for global citizenship. Posters urging Americans to "beat back the Hun," accompanied by a monstrous picture of a German soldier, appeared in World War I. Songs such as "We have to slap the dirty little Jap" were popular in World War II. We are ashamed of them now. What was the object of these posters, songs, and slogans? Pretending that we never used such devices or worrying that reviving them for present criticism will reopen old wounds is almost certainly a mistake. Citizens must face their own histories and their vulnerability to indoctrination.

Propaganda works in two directions. It makes the enemy into monsters and one's own military into heroes. On the latter, students should be asked to consider whether young people automatically become heroes by putting on uniforms and being sent into battle. How is it that in times of peace many of these young people are regarded as poor students who enter the military because they need discipline and direction? Students should read Kipling's *Barrack-Room Ballads* and discuss ways in which propaganda creates heroes. And what is a hero? This question—like, What is a patriot?—should be given serious attention. Students should also discuss the hypocrisy of the civilian population that so adores "our boys" in wartime and shows so little regard for them as struggling students.

Possibly the most important issue for high school juniors and seniors to study and discuss is the psychology of war. Does everyone hate war? In the last 2 years, Americans have heard our leaders say repeatedly, No one wants war! The implication is that "we" will fight only if war is forced on us. Although it is true that national leaders have sometimes tried to avoid war, it is clearly not true that no one wants war. Greedy and power-hungry people often want war, because war offers both money and power. In addition, there are those who thirst for the glory and excitement of war.

Anthony Swofford, a marine, contrasts the effects of war films on civilians and military men:

> Mr. and Mrs. Johnson in Omaha or San Francisco or Manhattan will watch the films and weep and decide once and for all that war is inhumane and terrible . . . [We] watch the same films and are excited by them, because the magic brutality of the films celebrates the terrible and despicable beauty of [our] fighting skills. Fight, rape, war, pillage, burn. Filmic images of death and carnage are pornography for the military man. (2003, 6–7)

Surely many military people reject Swofford's view. But many boys feel as he does, and even those who do not may lose control of their moral resources in the heat of combat. Soldiers of all nations have committed terrible acts in war. Jonathan Glover has written about the horrors of 20th-century warfare. He quotes a Soviet soldier who served in Afghanistan: "We're invited to speak in schools, but what can we tell them? Not what war is really like, that's for sure . . . I can't very well tell the school kids about collections of dried ears and other trophies of war, can I?" (quoted in Glover 2000, 168).

Small children shouldn't hear such things, but older teens about to graduate from high school *should* hear these things, and they should learn that American veterans of Vietnam can match these horror tales—right down to the necklaces of dried human ears. Can we claim to have educated our children if we send them into the world without a knowledge of what may happen to them in war?

Most high school students are required to read at least part of Homer's *Iliad*. They should read and reflect on the parts in which Achilles mercilessly kills a young Trojan soldier who is begging for his life. They should hear the warriors on both sides taunting each other with accusations of cowardice. And they should be encouraged to ask themselves: Might I kill a helpless enemy if I had just seen my best friend killed or my city destroyed, or if I had been threatened with shame for being too soft?

How have some soldiers managed to sustain their moral resources when others have given way to cruelty and mayhem? Tony Hillerman (whose Navajo mystery stories students might enjoy) describes his own experience as a young infantryman in WWII. He comments, "One finds humanitarians in every army and brutes as well" (2001, 100), and he recounts vivid stories of the activities of both.

After reading many accounts of military action, students may suspect that the division between humanitarians and brutes is fragile and depends more heavily than we would wish on circumstances. Preparing students through study and open discussion cannot guarantee that they will not behave badly in horrible circumstances, but it may make such a descent into brutish behavior less likely. Better yet, it may convince some young people that war must be rejected as a means of resolving human conflict.

THE USE OF ART AND LITERATURE

Many educators advocate the use of art and literature in teaching for cultural sensitivity, moral reflection, and global understanding. However, in making this recommendation (which I endorse strongly), we must recognize that the case for art and literature in the formation of attitudes is ambiguous. Consider the statement quoted earlier in this chapter from Anthony Swofford, who claimed that he and his military comrades were excited and attracted by the depiction of war's horrors.

Virginia Woolf explored the possibility that fine, truthful literature and art might persuade the public against war. In 1938, she wrote:

> Is it not possible that if we knew the truth about war, the glory of war would be scotched and crushed where it lies curled up in the rotten cabbage leaves of our prostituted fact-purveyors; and if we knew the truth about art . . . the enjoyment and practice of art would become so desirable that by comparison the pursuit of war would be a tedious game for elderly dilettantes . . . ? (1966, 97)

More than 60 years later, Susan Sontag (2003) has explored the same question and come to the conclusion that I think we must face. There simply is no guarantee that even the most powerful art will have desirable moral effects.

In schooling, perhaps much depends on how teachers use literature. Certainly if the teacher's attention is only on technique, figures of speech, the identification of great writers and the titles of their books, and the names of chief characters, students are not likely to delve deeply into moral questions. Indeed, teachers often avoid controversial moral questions or cut short discussion of them (Simon 2001). If we want to encourage reflection and critical thinking, we have to entrust our students with the full discussion of moral issues, and we have to plan our lessons with moral/existential questions in mind.

In reading Ralph Ellison's *Invisible Man* (1952), there should be pauses to explore how it might feel to be ignored and treated like someone barely human. How would *you* feel if you were a bright, conscientious student dismissed for a tragicomic event beyond your control and then given (as a compensation) a letter of introduction that, instead of promoting your cause (as you've been led to believe), is designed to ruin your chances entirely?

Is it possible that a little black girl could suppose that her only hope for a decent future lay in God's granting her blue eyes? Who can get through Toni Morrison's *The Bluest Eye* (1970) without tears? But there has to be time for reflection: What if this were my life? The challenge to teachers is to use literature for moral reflection without losing sight of the authors' genius. We do not have to choose between one aim and another.

There are many novels that can help students to feel what people have gone through as a result of discrimination. Laura Hobson's *Gentleman's Agreement* (1947) and *First Papers* (1964) portray prejudice against Jews, and *First Papers* also provides a historically accurate and interesting account of life in America just before World War I. The stories of Isaac Bashevis Singer (see Singer 1983) also contribute to both historical and cultural knowledge of Jewish experience.

The novels of Amy Tan (*The Joy Luck Club*, 1989; *The Bonesetter's Daughter*, 2001) tell us much about the culture of Chinese immigrants in America and, at the same time, invite discussion about the status of women in Chinese tradition. Many students will be asked to read Pearl Buck's *The Good Earth* (1933), but they should also be encouraged to read *The Exile* (1936), Buck's biography of her mother and *Fighting Angel* (1936), the biography of her father. These two books reveal a significant gender gap in attitudes toward religion, children, and life itself. When a book is chosen to induce discussion of cultural, gender, or religious differences, teachers should spend some time putting together a list of additional readings. Students can then be asked to report, individually or in groups, on these supplementary readings, thus enhancing the experience of everyone.

There are thousands of books in my house, and several hundred of them could be useful as prologues to discussion on cultural, religious, and gender differences. I've mentioned but a few as examples. We might add Louise Erdrich's Native American novels (e.g., Erdrich 1984, 1988, 1994, 1996); Wallace Stegner's *Angle of Repose* (1971) and his biography of John Wesley Powell on the subject of place; and John Knowles's *A Separate Peace* (1960) and *Peace Breaks Out* (1981) on the topics of war, masculinity, and competition.

We could certainly put together long lists of readings on every topic considered in this volume. But what should teachers do with these lists? Some teachers spend weeks dissecting a single novel, and the end result is often boredom and a reduced interest in reading. Among my books are many autobiographies, and almost all of them attest to the negative effects of studying literature in school. Many of the writers were avid readers, but they chose their own reading—sometimes to escape the boredom of classroom analysis. Thus it seems that teacher-led, meticulous analysis may be counterproductive.

But surely some teacher guidance is required. Not too much! Katherine Simon (2001) reports on a teacher who supplied 230 study questions for a book of about as many pages. Predictably, students concentrated on "getting the answers" to the teacher's questions and forgot about the moral issues in the book.

If literature is to be effective in shaping moral and social attitudes, it has to affect readers—make them feel something. And it is those feelings that lead to lively discussion and reflection. Perhaps analysis should be directed by expressions of student feeling. Teachers could give very brief directions as students start to read: How would you feel if you were in the position of one or other of the main characters? What would you do? Why? If your feelings or decisions would be different from those of the character(s), what do you think accounts for the difference? Analysis should then proceed on the basis of student interest and involvement.

If English teachers often sacrifice the deepest rewards of literature for details that will surely be forgotten, other teachers neglect literature entirely. But there are novels, biographies, poetry, and essays relevant to all school subjects, and these could be used to encourage the habits of mind and heart we have been discussing.

Teachers, too, can be moved and changed by varied and sensitive reading. Consider how teachers might rethink what they are doing after reading Günter Grass's *Crabwalk* (2002). The narrator, Paul Pokriefke, is a contemporary German journalist whose mother has continually urged him to write the story of a ship, the *Wilhelm Gustloff*. He is the right person to write it, she insists, because he was born as the *Gustloff* was sunk by a Russian submarine toward the end of World War II. Some 9,000 people, many of them children, died; the newborn (or unborn) Paul and his mother were among the few survivors. Paul procrastinates. He marries, has a son, and is separated from his wife. She allows their teenage son, Konny, to join his grandmother, and from her, Konny learns the story of the *Gustloff*; that is, he learns a version of the story that sends him on a quest. He learns that the *Gustloff* was named for a Nazi functionary who was assassinated before World War II by a Jew, David Frankfurter, who acted in the hope of arousing fellow Jews to the rising danger they faced. Tried in Switzerland, Frankfurter was imprisoned for some years and then deported to Israel.

Konny pursues this story with academic diligence but with no real adult guidance, only the slanted tales of his grandmother. He writes a paper on the events, but his teachers will not allow him to present or discuss it. He starts an Internet conversation with others on the topic and engages in heated (but oddly friendly) debate with a boy named David, ostensibly a Jew who defends Frankfurter's act. Eventually the two boys meet and Konny kills David. He uses four shots, just as Frankfurter did on Gustloff. As Frankfurter said that he shot Gustloff because "I am a Jew," Konny says, "I shot [him] because I am a German—and because the eternal Jew spoke through David" (Grass 2002, 204). Because he is a juvenile, Konny gets a relatively light prison term.

Paul tries to make up for his years of parental neglect by visiting Konny regularly in prison. After many failed attempts at communication, Paul senses a breakthrough when Konny smashes an elaborate model of the *Gustloff*. But then he discovers a new Web site:

Campaigning for someone whose conduct and thinking it held up as exemplary, someone whom the hated system had for that very reason locked up. "We believe in you, we will wait for you, we will follow you . . ." And so on and so forth. It doesn't end. Never will it end. (234)

As a teacher, I was deeply moved by this story. Might things have turned out differently if Konny's teachers had allowed free debate and offered an honest and friendly revision of the stories his grandmother told? What was Konny to think about the honesty of the official adult world when even the sinking of the *Gustloff*—the worst maritime disaster in history—had been long suppressed? How was he—a bright boy, but just a boy—to understand the influence of German guilt on the repression of all accounts of German suffering in and after World War II? Obviously, Grass, a proven anti-Nazi, has begun to ask himself the same questions, and so had his recently deceased compatriot W. G. Sebald (2003).

Our hope in writing this book is that the hatred, distrust, ignorance, and sense of national superiority that have characterized past history will end. To contribute to that end, we teachers must engage our students in open, honest dialogue—sharing, guiding, and staying with them as they struggle with problems we have not solved.

References

Aber, J. L., Brown J. L., & Henrich, C. C. (1999). *Teaching conflict resolution: An effective school-based approach to violence prevention*. New York: Columbia University, National Center for Children in Poverty

Allendoefer, C. (2001). Ethnic identity under construction: Vietnamese students in an English as a second language classroom. In *Negotiating transnationalism: Selected papers on refugees and immigrants*, M. Hopkins and N. Wellmeier, eds., Volume IX, 97–122. Arlington, VA: American Anthropological Association.

Allison, D. (1994). *Skin: Talking about sex, class, and literature*. Ithaca, NY: Firebrand Books

Andrzejewski, J., & Alessio, J. (1999). Education for global citizenship and social responsibility. University of Vermont: *Progressive Perspectives* 1(2): 1–10.

Armstrong, D. G. (2003). *Curriculum today*. Upper Saddle River, NJ: Merrill Prentice Hall.

Ayers, W. (1998). A dream that keeps on growing—Myles Horton and Highlander. In *Teaching for social justice*, W. Ayers, J. A. Hunt, and T. Quinn, eds., 150–156. New York: New Press.

Barnes, D. (1992). *From communication to curriculum*, 2nd ed. Portsmouth, NH: Boynton/Cook Publishers.

Basso, K. (1996). *Wisdom sits in places*. Albuquerque: University of New Mexico Press.

Beevor, A. (2002). *The fall of Berlin 1945*. New York: Viking.

Berlin, I. (1969). *Four essays on liberty*. Oxford: Oxford University Press.

Berman, S. (1997). *Children's social consciousness and the development of social responsibility*. Albany: State University of New York Press.

Berry, W. (1995). *Another turn of the crank*. Washington, D.C.: Counterpoint.

———. (1996). *The unsettling of America*. San Francisco: Sierra Club. Original work published 1977.

Bigelow, B., & Peterson, B., eds. (2002). *Rethinking globalization: Teaching for justice in an unjust world*. Milwaukee: Rethinking Schools.

Billington, R. A. (1966). *The historian's contribution to Anglo-American misunderstanding*. New York: Hobbs, Dorman.

Bracey, G. W. (2003). Tips for readers of research: Numbers versus percentage. *Phi Delta Kappan* January 2003: 410–411.

Brion-Meisels, S. (1995). *Constructing the peaceable school: First steps on the journey*. Unpublished manuscript.

Brophy, J., ed. (1993). *Advances in research on teaching, Volume 4: Case studies of teaching and learning in social studies.* Greenwich, CT: JAI Press.

Browne, J. (2002). *Charles Darwin: The power of place.* New York: Alfred A. Knopf.

Buber, M. (1965). *Between man and man.* New York: Macmillan.

Buchwald, E., Fletcher, P. R., & Roth, M., eds. (1993). *Transforming a rape culture.* Minneapolis: Milkweed Editions.

Buck, P. (1933). *The good earth.* New York: The Modern Library.

———. (1936). *The exile.* New York: Collier.

———. (1936). *Fighting angel.* New York: Reynal & Hitchcock.

Carlsson-Paige, N., & Levin, D. (1992). Making peace in violent times: A constructivist approach to conflict resolution. *Young Children*, National Association for the Education of Young Children, (48, November): 4–13.

———. (1998). *Before push comes to shove: Building conflict resolution skills with children.* St. Paul, MN: Red Leaf Press.

Carnegie Corporation & Center for Information and Research in Civic Learning. (2003). *The civic mission of schools.* New York: Author.

Carson, R. (1962). *Silent spring.* Boston: Houghton Mifflin.

Casey, E. S. (1993). *Getting back into place.* Bloomington: Indiana University Press.

Center for Information and Research in Civic Learning (CIRCLE). (2002). *Early 2002 survey of young Americans aged 15–25.* New York: Carnegie Corporation and CIRCLE.

———. (2003). *The civic mission of schools.* New York: Carnegie Corporation of New York and The Center for Information and Research on Civic Learning and Engagement (CIRCLE).

Children's Defense Fund. (2001). *The state of America's children yearbook 2002.* Washington, DC: Author.

Consensus Building Institute (CBI). (2000). *Teaching the mutual gains approach.* Cambridge, MA: Author.

———. (2004). *Workable peace: Teaching young people and educators to manage conflict between groups.* Cambridge, MA: Author.

Cornbleth, C. (2002). "What it means to be an American." Paper presented at the annual meeting of the American Educational Research Association, New Orleans.

Cotton, K. (1996). *Educating for citizenship.* School Improvement Research Series IX. Chicago: North West Regional Education Laboratory.

Crawford, D., & Bodine, R. (1996). *Conflict resolution education: A guide to implementing programs in schools, youth-serving organizations, and community and juvenile justice settings.* Washington, DC: Office of Juvenile Justice and Delinquency Prevention, U.S. Department of Justice, and Office of Elementary and Secondary Education, U.S. Department of Education.

Crenson, M., & Ginsberg, B. (2002). *Downsizing democracy: How America sidelined its citizens and privatized its public.* Baltimore: Johns Hopkins University.

Daly, M. (1974). *Beyond God the father.* Boston: Beacon Press.

Day, D. (1952). *The long loneliness.* San Francisco: Harper & Row.

Delgado, R., ed. (1995). *Critical race theory: The cutting edge.* Philadelphia: Temple University Press.

Derrida, J. (1978). *Writing and difference*, trans. A. Bass. Chicago: University of Chicago Press.

Dewey, J. (1916). *Democracy and education*. New York: Macmillan.

———. (1930). *Human nature and conduct*. New York: Modern Library.

———. (1938). *Experience and education*. New York: Macmillan.

———. (1969). What is social study? In *Teaching the social studies: What, why, and how*, eds., R. E. Gross, W. E. McPhie, and J. R. Fraenkel. Scranton, PA: International Textbook Company. Original edition, 1938.

———. (1991a). *How we think*. Amherst, NY: Prometheus Books. Original edition, 1910.

———. (1991b). The challenge of democracy to education. In *The later works, Vol. 11, 1925–1953*, eds., J. A. Boydston. Carbondale, IL: Southern Illinois University Press. Original edition, 1937.

Donahue-Keegan, D., & LaRusso, M. (1999). *Independent evaluation of the workable peace project*. Cambridge, MA: Harvard Graduate School of Education (unpublished report available from Consensus Building Institute, Cambridge, MA).

Duncan, C. M. (1999). *Worlds apart: Why poverty persists in rural America*. New Haven: Yale University Press.

Earth Council. (2002). *The earth charter: Values and principles for a sustainable future*. San Jose, Costa Rica: The Earth Council.

Eck, D. (1993). *Encountering God: A spiritual journey from Bozeman to Banaras*. Boston: Beacon Press.

———. (2001). *A new religious America: How a "Christian country" has become the world's most religiously diverse nation*. San Francisco: HarperCollins.

Egan, K. (1999). *Children's minds, talking rabbits, & clockwork oranges*. New York: Teachers College Press.

———. (2003). Start with what student knows or with what the student can imagine? *Phi Delta Kappan* 84(6): 443–445.

Eisner, E. W. (1972). *Educating artistic vision*. New York: Macmillan.

Elder, J. (1998). *Reading the mountains of home*. Cambridge: Harvard University Press.

Elkind, D. (1998). *All grown up and no place to go*. Cambridge, MA: Perseus Books.

Ellis, W. S., & Turnley, D. (1990). A Soviet sea lies dying. *National Geographic* 177(2): 73–93.

Ellison, R. (1952). *Invisible man*. New York: Random House.

Elshtain, J. B. (1987). *Women and war*. New York: Basic Books.

Epstein, T. (2001). Adolescents' perspectives on racial diversity in U.S. history: Case studies from an urban classroom. *American Educational Research Journal* 37: 185–214.

Erdrich, L. (1984). *Love medicine*. New York: Holt, Rinehart and Winston.

———. (1988). *Tracks*. New York: Henry Holt.

———. (1994). *Bingo palace*. New York: HarperCollins.

———. (1996). *Burning love*. New York: HarperCollins.

Farman Farmaian, S. (1992). *Daughter of Persia*. New York: Doubleday.

Fisher, R. (1993). The potential for peacebuilding: Forging a bridge from peacekeeping to peacemaking. *Peace and Change* 18(3, July): 247–266.

————. (2000). Intergroup conflict. In *The handbook of conflict resolution*, eds. M. Deutsch and P. Coleman, 166–184. San Francisco: Jossey-Bass.

Fisher, R., & Ury, W. (1983). *Getting to yes*. New York: Penguin Books.

Ford, L. R. (2000). *The spaces between buildings*. Baltimore: Johns Hopkins.

Foster, S., & Nicholls, J. (2003). *Portrayal of America's role during World War II: An analysis of school history textbooks from England, Japan, Sweden, and the U.S.A.* Paper read at American Educational Research Association, April, Chicago.

Frazer, J. G. (1951). *The golden bough*. New York: Macmillan.

Garbarino, J. (1995). *Raising children in a socially toxic environment*. San Francisco, CA: Jossey-Bass, Inc.

Gardner, H. (1993). *Frames of mind: The theory of multiple intelligences*. New York: Basic Books.

Glendon, M. A. (2001). *A world made new: Eleanor Roosevelt and the making of the Universal Declaration of Human Rights*. New York: Random House.

Glover, J. (2000). *Humanity: A moral history of the 20th century*. New Haven: Yale University Press.

Goodlad, J. (1984). *A place called school: Prospects for the future*. Hightstown, NJ: McGraw Hill.

Grass, G. (2002). *Crabwalk*, trans. Krishna Winston. Orlando: Harcourt.

Grissell, E. (2001) *Insects and gardens: In pursuit of a garden ecology*. Portland, OR: Timber Press.

Gross, R. E. (1958). United States history. In *Educating citizens for democracy*, eds. R. E. Gross and L. D. Zeleny. New York: Oxford University Press.

Hague Appeal for Peace. (2001). *Hague Appeal for Peace: Global campaign for peace education*. The Hague, Netherlands: Author.

Halstead, T. (2003). The American paradox. *Atlantic Monthly*, Jan./Feb. 2003: 123–125.

Harding, V. (1990). *Hope and history: Why we must share the story of the movement*. Maryknoll, NY: Orbis Books.

Hardy, Thomas. (n.d.). *The return of the native*. New York: Library Publications. Original work published in 1878.

Harris, I., & Morrison, M. L. (2003). *Peace education*, 2nd ed. Jefferson, NC: McFarland.

Harrison-Wong, C. (2003). *Educational significance of how U.S. history textbooks treat Hiroshima*. Ed.D. diss., Columbia University, New York.

Hedges, C. (2002). War is a force that gives us meaning. *Amnesty Now* Winter 2002: 10–13.

Hillerman, T. (2001). *Seldom disappointed*. New York: HarperCollins.

Hobson, L. (1947). *Gentleman's agreement, a novel*. New York: Simon and Schuster.

————. (1964). *First papers*. New York: Random House.

Hofstadter, R. (1967). *The American political tradition and the men who made it*. London: Jonathan Cape.

Horowitz, D. (1985). *Ethnic groups in conflict*. Berkeley: University of California Press.

James, W. (1929). *The varieties of religious experience*. New York: Modern Library. Original published 1902.

Jenkins, P. (2002). *The next Christendom: The coming of global Christianity*. New York: Oxford University Press.

Jervis, R. (1978). Cooperation under the security dilemma. *World Politics* 30 (2, January): 167–213.

Johnson, D., & Johnson, R. (1994). Constructive conflict in the schools. *Journal of Social Issues* 50(1): 117–138.

Juergensmeyer, M. (2000). *Terror in the mind of God: The rise of Religious violence*. Berkeley: University of California Press.

Jung, C. G. (1969). *Collected works*, vol. 2. Princeton: Princeton University Press.

Kahn, P. (1999). *The human relationship with nature*. Cambridge, MA: MIT Press.

Kaufman, S. J. (2002). *Modern hatreds: The symbolic politics of ethnic war*. Ithaca: Cornell University Press.

Keller, C. (1993). Talk about the weather. In *Ecofeminism and the sacred*, ed. Carol J. Adams, 30–49. New York: Continuum.

Kelman, H. (1997). Social-psychological dimensions of international conflict. In *Peacemaking in international conflict: Methods and techniques*, eds. I. W. Zartman and J. L Rasmussen, pp. 197–237. Washington, D.C.: U.S. Institute of Peace Press.

Kilson, M. (1998). In defense of Black race redemption discourse: Nationalism vs. neoliberalism. Paper presented at the Third Annual W. E. B. DuBois and the Construction of Social Scientific Knowledge Conference, April 10–11, Philadelphia.

Kimball, C. (2002). *When religion becomes evil*. San Francisco: HarperCollins.

Knitter, P. F., & Muzaffar, C., eds. (2002). *Subverting greed: Religious perspectives on the global economy*. Maryknoll, NY: Orbis Books in Association with the Boston Research Center for the 21st Century.

Knowles, J. (1960). A separate peace. New York: Macmillan.

———. (1981). *Peace breaks out*. New York: Holt, Rinehart and Winston.

Kohn, A. (1999). *The schools our children deserve*. Boston, MA: Houghton Mifflin.

———. (2001). Presentation at Lesley University's Peaceable Schools Summer Institute at Lesley University, Cambridge, MA.

———. (2001). "From compliance to community." Presentation, the Lesley University Peaceable Schools Summer Institute, June 29, Cambridge, MA.

Kozol, J. (1991). *Savage inequalities*. New York: Crown.

Krauss, R., & Morsella, E. (2000). Communication and conflict. In *The handbook of conflict resolution*, eds. M. Deutsch and P. Coleman, 131–143. San Francisco: Jossey-Bass.

Kriner, S. (2003). *In the news: Aral Sea ecological disaster causes humanitarian crisis* [World Wide Web]. http://www.redcross.org/news/in/asia/020410aral.html.

Kymlicka, W. (1995). *Multicultural citizenship*. Oxford: Oxford University Press.

———. (1998). Multicultural citizenship. In *The citizenship debates*, ed. G. Shafir, 167–188. Minneapolis: University of Minnesota Press.

Lake, D., & Rothchild, D. (1998). Spreading fear: The genesis of transnational ethnic conflict. In *The international spread of ethnic conflict*, eds. D. Lake and D. Rothchild, 3–32. Princeton: Princeton University Press.

Lane, R. E. (2000). *The loss of happiness in market democracies*. New Haven: Yale University Press.

Lantieri, L., & Patti, J. (1996). *Waging peace in our schools*. Boston, MA: Beacon Press.

Lax, D., & Sebenius, J. (1993). The power of alternatives or the limits to negotiation. In *Negotiation theory and practice*, eds. J. W. Breslin and J. Rubin, 97–114. Cambridge, MA: Program on Negotiation Books.

Levin, D. (2003). *Teaching young children in violent times: Building a peaceable classroom*. Cambridge, MA: Educators for Social Responsibility.

Lickona, T. (1991). *Educating for character*. New York: Bantam Books.

Lieber, C. M. (1998). *Conflict resolution in the high school*. Cambridge, MA: Educators for Social Responsibility.

———. (2002). *Partners in learning*. Cambridge, MA: Educators for Social Responsibility.

Loges, W. E., & Kidder, R. M. (1997). *Global values, moral boundaries: A pilot study*. Camden, ME: The Institute of Global Ethics.

Long, H. M., & King, R. N. (1964). *Improving the teaching of world affairs: The Glens Falls story*. Washington, D.C.: National Council for the Social Studies.

Lustig, I. (2001). *The effects of studying distant conflicts on the perception of a proximal one*. Master's thesis, University of Haifa.

Makiguchi, T. (2002). *A geography of human life*. [English reprint, edited by D. M. Bethel]. San Francisco: Caddo Gap Press. Original work in Japanese, published in 1903.

Markham, E. (1899). *The man with the hoe and other poems*. New York: Doubleday McClure Co.

Marsden, W. E. (2000). Geography and two centuries of education for peace and international understanding. *Geography* 85(4): 289–302.

———. (2001). *The school textbook: Geography, history, and social studies*. London: Woburn Press.

Marshall, T. H. (1964). *Class, citizenship, and social development*. Garden City, NY: Doubleday.

McNeil, L. (1986). *Contradictions of control*. New York: Routledge.

Michigan State Department of Education. (2003). *Social studies* [World Wide Web]. Michigan Department of Education c. 2001 [cited May 18 2003]. Available from http://www.michigan.gov/mde/0,1607,7–140–6525_6530_6568-19452—,00.html.

Miller, J. B. (1976). *Toward a new psychology of women*. Boston: Beacon Press.

Morrison, T. (1970). *The bluest eye*. New York: Holt, Rinehart and Winston.

Moynahan, B. (2002). *The faith: A history of Christianity*. New York: Random House.

Nabhan, G. P., & Trimble, S. (1994). *The geography of childhood: Why children need wild places*. Boston: Beacon Press.

Naimark, N. M. (2002). *Fires of hatred: Ethnic cleansing in twentieth-century Europe*. Cambridge: Harvard University Press.

Nash, R. (2001). Constructing a spirituality of teaching: A spiritual perspective. *Religion & Education*, Spring, 2001: 1–20.

———. (2002). *Spirituality, ethics, religion, and teaching: A professor's journey*. New York: Peter Lang.

National Center for Children in Poverty (NCCP). (2002). *Low income children in the United States: A brief demographic profile* (fact sheet). New York: Trustees of Columbia University. Available at www.nccp.org

National Public Radio. (2003). *The citizen student*. January. Washington, DC: Author.

Neill, M., & Gayler, K. (2001). Do high-stakes graduation tests improve learning outcomes? Using state-level NAEP data to evaluate the effects of mandatory graduation tests. In *Raising standards or raising barriers? Inequality and high-stakes testing in public education*, eds. G. Orfield and M. L. Kornhaber, 107–125. New York: The Century Foundation Press.

New York State Education Department. (1990s). *Social studies resource guide with core curriculum*. Albany: Author. Available at http://www.emsc.nysed.gov/ciai/socst/ssrg.html

Noddings, N. (1984). *Caring: A feminine approach to ethics and moral education*. Berkeley: University of California Press.

———. (1993). *Educating for intelligent belief and unbelief*. New York: Teachers College Press.

———. (2002). *Starting at home: Caring and social policy*. Berkeley: University of California Press.

———. (2003a). *Happiness and education*. New York: Cambridge University Press.

———. (2003b). Is teaching a practice? *Journal of the Philosophy of Education Society of Great Britain* 37 (2): 241–251.

Nord, W. (1995). *Religion & American education: Rethinking a national dilemma*. Chapel Hill: The University of North Carolina Press.

Oliver, D. W., & Shaver, J. P. (1966). *Teaching public issues in the high school*. Boston: Houghton Mifflin.

Ong, A. (1999). *Flexible citizenship: The cultural logics of transnationality*. Raleigh: Duke University Press.

Operation Respect, Inc. and Educators for Social Responsibility. (2000). *Don't laugh at me*. New York: Operation Respect.

Orwell, G. (1941). *The lion and the unicorn*. London: Secker and Warburg.

Parsons, T. (1965). Full citizenship for the Negro American? A sociological problem. *Daedalus* 94 (4): 1009–1054.

Pellow, D. N. (2002). *Garbage wars: The struggle for environmental justice in Chicago*. Cambridge, MA: MIT Press.

Pew Research Center for the People and the Press. (2003). [Pew Global Attitudes Project.] *Views of a changing world: How global publics view war in Iraq, democracy, Islam and governance, globalization*. Washington, DC: Author. Available at http://people-press.org/reports/.

Piaget, J. (1952). *The child's conception of number*. London: Humanities Press.

Platt, K. (1996). Places of experience and the experience of place. In *The Longing for Home*, ed. Leroy S. Rouner, 112–127. Notre Dame: University of Notre Dame Press.

Pollan, M. (1991). *Second nature*. New York: Delta.

———. (2001). *The botany of desire*. New York: Random House.

Pope, D. C. (2001). *"Doing school": How we are creating a generation of stressed out, materialistic, and miseducated students*. New Haven: Yale University Press.

Raider, E. (1995). Conflict resolution training in schools: translating theory into applied skills. In *Conflict, cooperation, & justice*, ed. J. Rubin, 93–121. San Francisco: Jossey-Bass.

Reardon, B.A. (1985). *Sexism and the war system*. New York: Teachers College Press.

Reich, R. (2002). *Bridging liberalism and multiculturalism in American education.* Chicago: University of Chicago Press.

Reisner, M. (1993). *Cadillac desert: The American west and its disappearing water.* New York: Penguin Books.

Ricoeur, P. (1969). *The symbolism of evil.* Boston: Beacon Press.

Rosaldo, R. (1997). Cultural citizenship, inequality, and multiculturalism. In *Latino cultural citizenship: Claiming identity, space, and rights,* eds. W. Flores and R. Benmayor, 27–38. Boston: Beacon Press.

Rubin, J., Pruitt, D., & Kim, S. H. (1994). *Social conflict: Escalation, stalemate and settlement,* 2nd ed. New York: McGraw Hill.

Ruddick, S. (1989). *Maternal thinking: Towards a politics of peace.* Boston: Beacon Press.

Rugg, H. (1941). *That men may understand: An American in the long armistice.* New York: Doubleday, Doran.

Schapiro, J. S. (1953). *Modern and contemporary European history (1815–1952).* Cambridge: The Riverside Press.

Schelling, T. (1960). *The strategy of conflict.* Cambridge, MA: Harvard University Press.

Schlesinger, A. M. (1938). Introduction. In *School histories at war: A study of the treatment of our wars in the secondary school history books of the United States and in those of its former enemies,* by A. Walworth. Cambridge, MA: Harvard University Press.

Schlesinger, A. M., Jr. (1992). *The disuniting of America: Reflections on a multicultural society.* New York: W.W. Norton.

Schrijvers, P. (2002). *The GI war against Japan.* New York: New York University Press.

Sebald, W. G. (2003). *On the natural history of destruction,* trans. Anthea Bell. New York: Random House.

Sebenius, J. (1992). Negotiation analysis: A characterization and review. *Management Science* 38(1, January 1992): 18–39.

Simon, K. (2001). *Moral questions in the classroom.* New Haven: Yale University Press.

Singer, I. B. (1983). *The collected stories of Isaac Bashevis Singer.* New York: Noonday Press.

Singer, P. (2002). *One world: The ethics of globalization.* New Haven: Yale University Press.

Smith, A., & Czarra, F. (2003). Teaching in a global context. *ASCD Infobrief* 32: 1–12.

Smith-Christopher, D. L., ed. (2000). *Subverting hatred: The challenge of nonviolence in religious traditions.* Maryknoll, NY: Orbis Books in Association with the Boston Research Center for the 21st Century.

Snyder, H. (2002). [No title]. *Juvenile Justice Bulletin,* November: NCJ 191729. Washington, DC: Office of Juvenile and Delinquency Prevention. Available at http://www.ncjrs.org/html/ojjdp/jjbul2002_11_1/contents.html

Soley, M. (1996). If it's controversial, why teach it? *Social Education* January: 9–14.

Sontag, S. (2002). Looking at war. *New Yorker* December 9, 2002: 82–98.

———. (2003). *Regarding the pain of others.* New York: Farrar, Straus and Giroux.

Spindler, G., ed. (1987). *Education and cultural process: Anthropological approaches*, 2nd ed. Prospect Heights, IL: Waveland Press.

State Department of Education. (1988). *California history–social science framework*. Sacramento, CA: Author.

Stegner, W. (1971). *Angle of repose*. New York: Doubleday.

———. (1992). *Beyond the hundredth meridian: John Wesley Powell and the second opening of the West*. New York: Penguin Books. Original work published 1954.

Stein, S. (1993). *Noah's garden: Restoring the ecology of our own back yards*. Boston: Houghton Mifflin.

Steinberg, T. (2002). *Down to earth*. Oxford: Oxford University Press.

Stevahn, L. (1998). *Teaching all students constructive conflict resolution through academic coursework*. Reprinted with permission of the National Institute for Dispute Resolution's Forum, Volume 35 in www.ncip.org/articles/Coursework.html

Stiglitz, J. E. (2002). *Globalization and its discontents*. New York: W.W. Norton.

Susskind, L., & Corburn, J. (2000). Using simulations to teach negotiation: Pedagogical theory and practice. In *Teaching negotiation: Ideas and innovations*, ed. M. Wheeler, 285–310. Cambridge, MA: PON Books.

Susskind, L., McKearnan, S., & Thomas-Larmer, J., eds. (1999). *Consensus building handbook*. London: Sage Publications.

Swofford, A. (2003). *Jarhead*. New York: Scribner.

Tan, A. (1989). *The Joy Luck Club*. New York: Putnam.

———. (2001). *The bonesetter's daughter*. New York: Putnam.

Taylor, A. J. P. (1962). *The origins of the Second World War*. New York: Antheneum.

Tellis, A., Szayna, T., & Winnefeld, J. (1997). *Anticipating ethnic conflict*. Santa Monica, CA: RAND.

Thornton, S. J. (1991). Teacher as curricular-instructional gatekeeper in social studies. In *Handbook of research on social studies teaching and learning*, ed. J. P. Shaver. New York: Macmillan.

———. (2001a). Educating the educators: Rethinking subject matter and methods. *Theory into Practice* 40: 72–78.

———. (2001b). Legitimacy in the social studies curriculum. In *A century of study in education: The centennial volume*, ed. L. Corno. Chicago: National Society for the Study of Education.

———. (2004). Citizenship education and social studies curriculum change after 9/11. In *Social education in the twentieth century: Curriculum and context for citizenship*, eds. C. Woyshner, J. Watras, and M. S. Crocco. New York: Peter Lang.

True, M. (1995). *An energy field more intense than war*. Syracuse, NY: Syracuse University Press.

Turner, J. (1985). *Without God, without creed*. Baltimore: Johns Hopkins University Press.

Uchida, D., with Cetron, M. & McKenzie, P. (1996). *Preparing students for the 21st century*. Arlington, VA: American Association of School Administrators.

United Nations. (1959). *Declaration of the rights of the child*. Available at http://www.unhchr.ch/html/menu3/b/25.htm

United Nations. (1961). *How to plan and conduct model U.N. meetings*. New York: Oceana Publications.

Walter, E. V. (1988). *Placeways: A theory of the human environment*. Chapel Hill: University of North Carolina Press.

Walworth, A. (1938). *School histories at war: A study of the treatment of our wars in the secondary school history textbooks of the United States and its former enemies*. Cambridge: Harvard University Press.

Walzer, M. (1977). *Just and unjust wars*. New York: Basic Books.

Ward, D. R. (2002). *Water wars: Drought, flood, folly, and the politics of thirst*. New York: Penguin Putnam.

Watras, J. (2004). Historians and social studies educators, 1893–1998. In *Social education in the twentieth century: Curriculum and context for citizenship*, eds. C. Woyshner, J. Watras, and M. S. Crocco. New York: Peter Lang.

Weidensaul, S. (1999). *Living on the wind: Across the hemisphere with migratory birds*. New York: North Point Press.

Wesley, E. B. (1943). History in the school curriculum. *Mississippi Valley Historical Review* 29(4): 570.

Westbrook, R. (1991). *John Dewey and American democracy*. Ithaca, NY: Cornell University Press.

When children do the work. (1996). Oakland, CA: California Working Group. Video.

Whitehead, A. N. (1967). *The aims of education*. New York: Free Press. Original work published 1929.

Wiesel, E. (1996). Longing for home. In *The longing for home*, ed. Leroy S. Rouner, 17–29. Notre Dame: University of Notre Dame Press.

Wigginton, B. E., ed. (1968). *The Foxfire book*. New York: Anchor Books.

Wilkins, R. (2001). *Jefferson's pillow: Founding fathers and the dilemma of black patriotism*. New York: Beacon Press.

Willner M., Hero, G., & Weiner, J. (1995). *Global studies volume II*. New York: Barron's Educational Series, Inc.

Wilson, E. O. (2002). *The future of life*. New York: Alfred A. Knopf.

Wilson, W. (2003). *The fourteen points* [World WideWeb]. Brigham Young University Library, World War I Document Archive 1918 [cited May 16 2003]. Available from http://www.lib.byu..edu/~rdh/wwi/1918/14points.html.

Woolf, V. (1966). *Three guineas*. New York: Harcourt Brace. Originally published in 1938.

About the Contributors

Nancy Carlsson-Paige, Ed.D., is a professor of education at Lesley University and a co-founder, with Linda Lantieri, of Lesley's master's degree program in conflict resolution and peaceable schools. For more than 20 years, Nancy has been studying both the effects of violence on children's social development, and how children learn the ideas and skills for caring relationships and positive conflict resolution. Nancy has co-authored four books and many articles on topics such as violence in children's lives, media violence and its effects on children, how children learn the skills of conflict resolution, and the creation of peaceable school communities. She is also the author of *Best Day of the Week* (Redleaf Press, 1998), a children's book about conflict resolution. Nancy is a research affiliate at the Center for Peaceable Schools, which she helped to co-found at Lesley University, and is an advocate for healthier, more nonviolent schools and communities for all children.

David Fairman is Vice-President for International Programs at the Consensus Building Institute (CBI) and associate director of the MIT-Harvard Public Disputes Program. He was the founding director of CBI's Workable Peace program, and currently co-directs it. In addition, he facilitates consensus-building and mediates resolution of complex public policy and organizational issues. He also teaches negotiation, consensus-building, and mediation skills, and has authored numerous scholarly articles, consulting reports, and negotiation simulations. He is a member of the board and chairman of the Outreach Committee of the Alliance for International Conflict Resolution. He holds a Ph.D. in political science from MIT and a B.A in history and literature from Harvard College.

Gloria Ladson-Billings is a professor in the Department of Curriculum & Instruction at the University of Wisconsin-Madison and a former senior fellow in Urban Education at the Annenberg Institute for School Reform at Brown University. Her research interests concern the relationship between culture and schooling, particularly successful teaching and learning for African-American students. Her publications include *The Dreamkeepers: Successful Teachers of African American Children*, the *Dictionary of Multicultural*

Education (with Carl A. Grant), *Crossing Over to Canaan: The Journey of New Teachers in Diverse Classrooms* (May 2001), and numerous journal articles and book chapters. She was formerly the editor of the *Teaching, Learning & Human Development* section of the *American Educational Research Journal* and a member of several editorial boards including *Urban Education*, *Educational Policy*, and *The Journal of Negro Education*. She served as member-at-large on the American Education Research Association Council (2000–2003).

Linda Lantieri has over 30 years of experience in education as a teacher, administrator, university professor, and internationally known expert in social and emotional learning and conflict resolution. She serves as the founding director of the Resolving Conflict Creatively Program (RCCP) of Educators for Social Responsibility, which supports the program in 400 schools in the United States. She is also the director of the New York Satellite Office of the Collaborative for Academic, Social, and Emotional Learning (CASEL), whose central offices are at the University of Illinois at Chicago. Linda is co-author of *Waging Peace in Our Schools* (Beacon Press, 1996) and editor of *Schools With Spirit: Nurturing the Inner Lives of Children and Teachers* (Beacon Press, 2001).

Peggy McIntosh is the associate director of the Wellesley College Center for Research on Women and co-director, with Emily Style, of the National S.E.E.D. (Seeking Educational Equity and Diversity) Project on Inclusive Curriculum. McIntosh's research and writing on unearned privilege is available through the Working Paper Series published by the Wellesley Center and includes "White Privilege and Male Privilege: A Personal Account of Coming to See Correspondences through Work in Women's Studies" (1988) and "Interactive Phases of Curricular and Personal Re-vision with Regard to Race" (1990).

Robert Nash is currently a professor of Integrated Professional Studies at the University of Vermont, where he has taught for 35 years. He teaches courses in personal narrative writing, applied ethics, religious pluralism, philosophy of education, and higher education. He is the author of several books, chapters, monographs, and articles on a variety of educational topics. He has spoken on the issue of religious pluralism at conferences and colleges throughout the country during the last several years. He is on the editorial board of the *Journal of Religion & Education* and one of its frequent contributors. Professor Nash's books include *Answering the Virtuecrats: A Moral Conversation on Character Education* (Teachers College Press, 1997), *Religious Pluralism in the Academy: Opening the Dialogue* (Peter Lang, 2001), and *Spirituality, Ethics, Religion, and Teaching: A Professor's*

Journey (Peter Lang, 2002). His writing on religious pluralism has been featured twice in the *Chronicle of Higher Education* online.

Editor **Nel Noddings** is Lee L. Jacks Professor of Child Education Emerita, Stanford University. Her career has encompassed classroom teaching, school administration, and curriculum development and included scholarly work in educational philosophy and theory. Among Noddings's area of interest are the ethics of care, moral education, place-based education, and education for global citizenship. Her recent books include *The Challenge to Care in Schools* (1992), *Educating for Intelligent Belief or Unbelief* (1994), *Philosophy of Education* (1995), *Starting at Home* (2002), *Educating Moral People* (2002), and *Happiness and Education* (2003).

Stacie Nicole Smith is director of the Workable Peace project at the Consensus Building Institute, and also works as an Associate on other training, mediation, and facilitation projects. Prior to working at CBI, Ms. Smith taught integrated English and social studies in a public alternative school in New York City, where she integrated issues of group identity, intergroup conflict, human rights, and social justice. Ms. Smith completed her master's in the Teaching of Social Studies at Columbia Teachers College in 1996. She earned a B.A. with honors in American political and social theory at Brown University, where she also interned with the Coalition of Essential Schools.

Stephen J. Thornton received his Ph.D. from Stanford University and is associate professor of Social Studies and Education at Teachers College, Columbia University. He is currently working on a second edition of *The Curriculum Studies Reader* (Routledge, 1997) with David J. Flinders, and a new book on teachers' roles in social studies curriculum development. His recent publications appear in numerous education journals and anthologies and include "Legitimacy in the Social Studies Curriculum" in *Education Across a Century: The Centennial Volume* (National Society for the Study of Education, 2001) and "From Content to Subject Matter," *The Social Studies* (November/December 2001).

Index

DATE DUE